The Rosary Heals

Joyful, Luminous, Sorrowful, and Glorious Mysteries

Fr. Robert DeGrandis, S.S.J.
and
Eugene Peter Koshenina

Foreword

Twenty-five years ago the nation's best-seller was "The Relaxation Response," by Herbert Benson, M.D. In this book he states that stress is one of the greatest killers in our society, and then proceeds to show that meditation and prayer counteract stress. Many studies in recent years have added credence to his conclusions. A few doctors have even left their professions to become psychiatrists stating they preferred to treat the root causes rather than the symptoms.

Herbert Benson, M.D. goes on to state, "Sixty to ninety percent of visits to physicians are for conditions related to stress. The Relaxation Response counteracts the harmful effects of stress in a host of conditions, including: anxiety, mild and moderate depression, anger and hostility, hypertension, irregular heartbeat, pain, premenstrual syndrome, infertility, and many other stress-related illnesses." His answer to these maladies is meditation and prayer.

These rosary meditations are a wonderful "relaxation response" to many problems. As people use them, they will experience a new peace and health of body, mind, and spirit. Many great saints stated that their most powerful meditations came from reflecting on the life, passion, and death of Jesus.

Pope John Paul II said, "When it is recited well, the rosary leads one into the living experience of the divine mystery and brings to hearts, families and the whole community that peace which we need so much." On October 16, 2002, the pope proclaimed 2003 as the special year of the Rosary when he signed his apostolic letter, "Rosarium Virginis Mariae" ("The Rosary of the Virgin Mary"). May there be miracles of grace flowing from these pages as they are prayerfully read and meditated upon.

Fr. Robert DeGrandis, S.S.J.

Foreword

I truly enjoyed working on this book because my family loves Jesus and Mary and Joseph, and we wanted to know more about the mysteries of the Rosary. As a youngster, I prayed that Jesus would enlighten me with regard to these great mysteries. Over the decades, Jesus has answered that prayer. A year ago after I had prayed the Rosary, I was still very sad. Suddenly, I felt soft hands clasp mine. I looked down and saw Mary's hands lovingly placed around mine.

When we pray the Rosary intensely, we get much more in return than we could possibly give: great peace; a warm sense of well-being; and much more. The Rosary is one of the finest ways to escape the dismal events of our world. I pray that all who read this book will come to know the Holy Family better. Life was difficult in their day as poverty and civil unrest was widespread. Temple priests didn't help as they piled heavy burdens on Jewish backs with 613 Mosaic laws, many of which they didn't observe themselves. Yet the Holy Family courageously went about conducting their lives in an exemplary manner, living in charity and obedience to God and to the very temple in Jerusalem that was to condemn Jesus to death.

It is my hope that this book will enhance the prayer lives of individuals and prayer groups. Mary told the visionaries of Medugorje that we must pray, pray, pray! Unheard of blessings are being bestowed on people who pray these days because the world is in grave sin, and so much is needed to save souls. I thank my beautiful wife Chu for helping me so very much with this book, and with her I wish all of you a most holy and joyful life in Our Lord. May God continue to bless you in every way!

Eugene Peter Koshenina

Authors' Note

It is our observation that this book will be used in at least two different ways. First, it will be used to pray the Rosary. Secondly, it will be used for meditation. Therefore, it behooves us to explain the organization of this book to aid the reader.

Each of the mysteries (Joyful, Luminous, Sorrowful, and Glorious) of the Rosary in this book has two main parts: first, the scriptural theme of the mystery, the story of the mystery, reflection on the story, and a prayer; secondly, reflections of saints corresponding to each of the respective mysteries.

It is our desire that all of us recite the rosary daily and relive the vivid story events of the mysteries as we meditate on the life of Jesus. We commune with the saints as we sip on their insightful thoughts which follow each of the mysteries. As we do so we participate in the ministry of Jesus Christ Nazarene, who will lead us to peace and healing every day of our life.

Contents

THE JOYFUL MYSTERIES

First Joyful Mystery:

The Annunciation of Mary

And when the angel had come to her, he said, "Hail, full of grace, the Lord is with you. Blessed are you among women (Luke 1:28).

See Mary as she sweeps the floor in a room in the temple, singing softly to herself as she works alone. She is a girl of fifteen, unmarried, slim and pretty; she is around five feet four inches tall. She is in an outer room of the temple where she cleans and cooks and sews. Suddenly the room is bathed in brilliant light, and a being as bright as the sun appears in the midst. The being of light dims so Mary can see him comfortably, and he looks at Mary ever so lovingly. He announces that he is the angel Gabriel. Mary is stunned, but the angel reassures her as he begins to give her the good news. Gabriel smiles warmly at Mary and tells her the Lord is with her, that she has found favor with God.

Mary is somewhat troubled by the awesome visitor from heaven, and she wonders what kind of greeting this might be, or even if it might be the evil one in disguise! She ponders the situation as the angel Gabriel continues, telling her "the Holy Spirit will come upon you and the power of the most high will overshadow you (Lk 1:35)." Gabriel prophesies that she will give birth to a boy, and that He will be called Jesus, the Son of the Most High God. Gabriel tells Mary that the Lord God will give him the throne of his father David, and He will reign over the house of Jacob forever, that His kingdom will have no end.

Mary begins to understand that this is indeed the angel Gabriel, and that he is offering her the opportunity to give birth to the Messiah prophesied by Isaiah. This is the supreme honor sought by many women in Israel. Mary is being called to the greatest privilege in human history. She is deeply mystified. What should she do? She is already betrothed to a man named Joseph, a carpenter from Nazareth. What should she tell him? Her decision will change the course of human history and touch the lives of all peoples forever.

Mary knows God is calling her to the greatest human holiness known to mankind. She debates within herself: "What is my heavenly Father asking of me?" She thinks about the situation; but it is clear to her that she must trust in God, and she is eager to do whatever the Father asks of her. Thus, she humbly but firmly says to Gabriel, "I am the Lord's servant, may it be done to me as you have said (Luke 1:38)." This is the great Fiat, the great "yes" to God, the great promise to her heavenly Father that she will give birth to the child Jesus. Mary is promising that she will love and care for Jesus as her own son even though He belongs to God; for Jesus is God, the Eternal Father's only begotten Son.

Mary suddenly feels a great love from God, and this affirms that it is the angel Gabriel and that what she heard from the angel is true. She revels in her new knowledge that she will have a most special child through the power of the Holy Spirit. Mary feels that she is well prepared for her mission. Her mother and father, Anne and Joachim, had taught her much about the world, and everything they knew about God and the coming Messiah from biblical scrolls and tradition. Mary knows she will eventually have to tell Joseph about the visit of the angel Gabriel, and she prays that he will understand and accept the message of the angel.

As a young girl, Mary had pledged herself to God in the temple, praying that she would be allowed by God to remain totally dedicated to Him throughout her life. Will Joseph understand this and agree to it? Mary is presented with a great dilemma, to bear the child Jesus, and yet to take Joseph as her spouse. She wants to be betrothed, but not to be married as husband and wife; she wants to join her chastity to that of Joseph's.

Do you understand that you, too, are called like Mary to trust completely in God, to ascend to a higher state of holiness and sanctification? Have you responded by saying, "Yes" to your heavenly Father? To Mary? Do you say the Rosary daily? As you recite the Rosary, do you meditate a few minutes on each of the great mysteries? Hearing more about each of the great mysteries will increase your intimacy with Jesus, Mary, and Joseph!

Do you spend time with Jesus, do you listen to Him at least a few minutes after receiving the Eucharist? Do you give your problems to Jesus, and then abandon yourself to Him? That is your time to be with Jesus, to converse with Him. He is eager to help us. Let us praise Jesus for at least a few minutes afterwards. By so doing we will please Our Heavenly Father, and will thereby become more blessed before God and man.

Is it so very difficult to become holy? Is it questionable whether you can even get to heaven? No, holiness is just "trying to love the Lord Jesus and people as best you can." It is easy from that point of view. Simply do the best you can! That is all our Father asks of you. A single kind word can save a heart. St. Peter of Alcantara wrote, "He does much in the sight of God who does his best, be it ever so little." Heaven will be our sublime reward! What is your reply? Ask Jesus for the grace of holiness in this mystery.

Hail, Mary, full of grace; the Lord is with you. Blessed and most beautiful are you among women, and blessed is the fruit of your womb. Mary, in obedience to you and in honor of Your Son, I repeat over and over with the angels; "Praise be to Jesus, now and forever!"

Second Joyful Mystery
The Visitation

Elizabeth was filled with the Holy Spirit and cried out in a loud voice: "Blest are you among women and blest is the fruit of your womb (Luke 1:41-42)."

As Mary thinks about her elderly cousin Elizabeth with child in her sixth month, her heart tells her she must go to her cousin. So she tells Joseph to whom she is betrothed that she has to leave Nazareth to help her relative through childbirth. Joseph heartily agrees to her desire to aid her cousin, so he arranges for safe travel. He then helps Mary get ready for the trip.

A long journey through bandit-infested country brings Mary and Joseph to Jerusalem, which is near the small town where Zechariah lives. This is as far along the way as Joseph can go. He ensures Mary will be safe traveling with a party going in her direction, and he sees her off.

Mary arrives at the house of her cousin Elizabeth. Mary knocks at the door and Zechariah opens it, but he is unable to speak because he did not believe the angel Gabriel when he foretold the birth of John the Baptist. Mary enters the house of Zechariah and greets Elizabeth. Elizabeth welcomes her joyfully saying in a loud voice, "Blessed are you among women, and blessed is the child you will bear. How is it that the Mother of my Lord should come to me? As soon as the sound of your greeting reached my ears, the baby in my womb leaped for joy. Blessed is she who has believed that what the Lord has said to her will be accomplished."

And Mary said, "My soul glorifies the Lord and my spirit rejoices in God my Savior,

For He has been mindful of the humble state of His servant.

From now on all generations will call me blessed,

For the Mighty One has done great things for me – holy is His name.

His mercy extends to those who fear Him, from generation to generation.

He has performed mighty deeds with His arm;

He has scattered those who are proud in their inmost thoughts.

He has brought down rulers from their thrones but has lifted up the humble.

He has filled the hungry with good things but has sent the rich away empty.

He has helped His servant Israel, remembering to be merciful to Abraham and his descendants forever, even as He said to our fathers." (Luke 1:39-55)

Elizabeth marvels at Mary's canticle, still unaware of Mary's heavenly visit from the angel Gabriel. She is unaware that Mary, her very own cousin, has been chosen from all eternity to be the mother of the Messiah prophesied by Isaiah. But Mary is the servant of the Lord, and thus she helps Elizabeth through the birth of the precursor of the Christ, John the Baptizer. On the eighth day after John's birth they were to circumcise the child and name him Zechariah. But Elizabeth spoke loudly saying, "No! He is to be called John!" They ask for a sign from Zechariah. He asks for a tablet and writes, "His name is John." Immediately Zechariah's voice is restored and he glorifies God in a canticle of praise.

The neighbors are filled with awe, and the child John is the talk of the hill country. They all wonder about it, asking, "What then is this child going to be? For the Lord's hand was with him." Mary stays with Elizabeth for about three months, and then she returns to Nazareth. "And the child John grew and became strong in spirit, and he lived in the desert until he appeared publicly to Israel (Luke 1: 57-80)."

After Mary returned from ministering to her cousin Elizabeth, Joseph saw that she was with child. He was greatly troubled. But three days later an angel told Joseph in a dream that Mary was with child through the power of the Holy Spirit. Joseph believed the dream, and he was betrothed to Mary. Joseph smiled as he accepted Mary's request that she remain forever a virgin, and he became her most holy heroic guardian.

Let us meditate on the canticle of Mary. It contains the secrets to eternal life. Then ponder over the unusual decision of Mary to go, although already pregnant, on a long journey to help her cousin. How easy and explainable it would have been for her to refuse her heart. But Mary was always undaunted by hardship.

Are we spiritually strong like Mary? Do we help out when needed, or do we sometimes look for a "reasonable" way out?

Mary accepted the great hardship of carrying the baby that belonged to God, knowing that she would have to give up her son Jesus to cruel men. Will we sacrifice our own worldly desires to build up the kingdom of God, or will we be like Zechariah and question God's Word? Do we occasionally selectively distrust the word of God?

Think of the times you needed help and were refused by a family member or a friend, and you were "crushed." Reflect and see if there was a time when *you* refused to assist someone. Repent of that incident and forgive yourself, and also forgive the one who refused to come to your assistance. Ask Mary to pray that you can forgive all those people who neglected you in some way and did not give what you needed, even if they were your father and mother that were neglectful of you.

Lord, we pray for the grace of unconditional forgiveness of ourselves and others. Holy Mary, Mother of God, pray for us sinners, especially for those who are most in need of your mercy, now and at the hour of our deaths. Amen, Father. Amen, Son. Amen, Holy Spirit of God.

Third Joyful Mystery:

The Birth of Jesus

She gave birth to her first-born son and wrapped him in swaddling clothes and laid him in a manger, because there was no room for them in the place where travelers lodged (Luke 2:7).

In those days Caesar Augustus ordered a census to be taken. So Joseph began preparations to take Mary, who was with child, from their home in Nazareth to go and fulfill the requirements of Rome. Joseph and Mary packed the necessary provisions, and Joseph walked alongside Mary astride their donkey to the little town of Bethlehem.

Joseph and Mary loved this gentle sure-footed creature, and it carried Mary safely all the way to Bethlehem even though she was in her ninth month. When they reached Bethlehem they expected to find lodging, but the town was overflowing with travelers. There was no room in any of the inns or any other suitable place.

Joseph was tired and getting a little upset, as he had gone

from door to door all night trying to find a room, but with no success. As he would return to Mary astride their donkey, the sweet smile on Mary's face always warmed him and gave him back his peace, for she cheerfully accepted any hardship allowed by God. Mary knew well Joseph's distress but, rather than expressing regrets over their *apparent* misfortune, she simply praised God and went on with Joseph from place to place.

Joseph was by now fairly familiar with the town, so he felt he could probably find shelter in one of the buildings near the inns. It was so cold, and they hadn't slept for a couple of days. So when Joseph spotted a row of stables behind one of the inns, he looked at Mary's face ever so carefully, searching her innermost thoughts. Mary's warm smile showed him they must shelter themselves in one of these stables. They went all the way down the row until they finally found an unoccupied stable.

It was the last and poorest of the stables, the front made of wood with a cave in the rear. But Joseph and Mary and the donkey needed to get out of the cold wind and sleep. So Mary dismounted with Joseph's help, and Joseph took the cold hungry donkey inside, placing him between two oxen with another donkey alongside. Joseph hung his cloak over the door to block the wind, and then fed the donkey. The animals helped warm the drafty cave.

Joseph took some hay near the manger and made a bed for Mary. Then he started a fire. Mary unpacked the blankets and some honey bread to eat, and they gave thanks to God for their blessings. After eating they were both exhausted, so they lay down to pray and sleep. Joseph covered his eyes with his arms and prayed in very deep meditation, and Mary prayed with great intensity *and with growing excitement* knowing her time had arrived. As Mary prayed, countless angels began to congregate. They sang and prayed with Mary. To the singing of angels, Mary went into a joyous heavenly embrace and gave birth to Jesus, unseeable in a mist of brilliant light. Thus Mary brought forth her Son into a difficult world while in an icy, cold stable. But she was very happy because the angels were all around them, and Joseph was there to assist her if necessary. The joy of Jesus' birth wiped away the cold and inconveniences of the cave. The angelic singing was heavenly and it created a joyous, supernatural atmosphere. God spared Mary the pain of childbirth because she would undergo more suffering during Jesus' last three years on earth than anybody, other than Jesus, had or would ever suffer.

It was a great shock to the humanity of Jesus to descend from the bright celestial love of heaven to the cold dark earth. Mary suckled the crying hungry, cold child. Joseph heard the crying and saw the unusual fading light when he uncovered his eyes. He was startled at what was happening. He jumped up, saw the newborn baby, and excitedly made a little bed with straw in the manger right under the breath of an oxen deepest in the cave as it was the warmest place. Mary placed Jesus on His little bed. The straw and warm breath kept Jesus warm, and He quickly fell asleep. Joseph and Mary knelt and worshipped Jesus, the Son of the Most High God.

In the fields nearby shepherds were grazing their flocks. Huddled under blankets, they felt sheltered though the night was cold. Suddenly a great company of angels appeared to them, praising God and singing "Glory to God in the highest, and on earth peace to men on whom this favor rests (Luke 1:14)." We know from scripture how the shepherds were excited by the angelic singing and by their messages.

The shepherds left their flocks in the care of others and went and found the baby Jesus, and worshipped Him. But this was not the end of their loving ways. These were the same loyal shepherds who accompanied Jesus on the way of the cross; and they cried their saddest tears in deepest grief for the Holy Innocent Jesus whom they had worshipped as a little baby so many years earlier.

There is much to reflect on here. Joseph and Mary showed utmost patience even though they couldn't find suitable lodging. Do we remain cheerful and patient in adversity? Joseph and Mary lodged in the worst place in town. Do we seek royal quarters and regal company, or are we happy to be in any decent place and cheer up everyone we run into?

Joseph and Mary and the shepherds showed utmost faith *in adoring the infant* Jesus! Is our faith firm and resolute in the face of a doubting world? We must not kill our love of God through doubt! Our faith, to be true, must be bold! Do we proclaim Jesus to the world? Do we, like the shepherds of old, accompany Jesus on His way of the cross through meditation, sacrifice, and suffering?

How was your birth? Was there negativity in some way that adversely affected you through your mother? Was she in fear because she lost a child or was not married? Was your father absent when she gave birth? What was the negativity when you were born? The emotions of a mother profoundly influence her child. Ask Jesus to take you back to that time and heal any negative feelings that were communicated by your mother at your birth.

Baby Jesus, may Your Heavenly Father be my Father here on earth. Child Jesus, we believe in You, adore You, trust You, love You, and worship You; and we give You thanks for Your many blessings. Jesus, give us the grace to remain close to Your heart always. Thank You, little Lord Jesus.

Fourth Joyful Mystery

The Presentation of Jesus in the Temple

When the day came to purify them according to the law of Moses, the couple brought him up to Jerusalem so that he could be presented to the Lord, for it is written in the law of the Lord, "Every first-born male shall be consecrated to the Lord (Luke 2:22-23)."

Mary and Joseph were fully aware that Jesus *is* the Son of God. They had worshipped him as a newborn baby in the manger in Bethlehem that cold windy night He was born. In so many ways, Jesus had seemed just an ordinary baby, crying, suckling, and wetting. Unwavering faith was required of Mary and Joseph so that never for an instant would they forget that Jesus is God Almighty. This deep faith would serve them both so well throughout the remainder of their lives. In time, Joseph and Mary returned with Jesus to their home in Nazareth.

After circumcision and the purification time according to the Law of Moses had been completed, Mary and Joseph went to the temple in Jerusalem to present the baby Jesus to the Lord. They made the prescribed offering of two doves. A priest named Simeon and a prophetess named Anna had been waiting for the Messiah for many years, not knowing who His parents or he might be. They meet the Holy Family and are elated to see the Messiah prophesied so long ago by Isaiah. They greet the family of Jesus with great love and tenderness.

It had been revealed to Simeon years earlier that he would not die before he had seen the Father's *Christ*, His *Anointed One*. Simeon recognizes that *this is* the Christ, so he takes the child Jesus in his arms and praises God saying, "… my eyes have seen your salvation…a light for revelation to the Gentiles and for glory to your people Israel." Simeon adds, "This child is destined to be the cause of rising and falling of many, and to be a sign that will be spoken against, so that the thoughts of many hearts will be revealed. And a sword will pierce your own soul also (Luke 2:21-35)."

"A sword will pierce your own soul also!" Was this not prophetic? Mary was granted the grace to suffer Christ's passion, and in a different way the lance of the Roman Commander Longinus was to penetrate the immaculate hearts of Jesus and Mary. As decades and centuries went by, nations rose and fell, and all of the words of Luke were fulfilled.

The prophetess Anna worshipped day and night in the Temple. Following Simeon, she came up to Jesus, gave thanks to God, and spoke about the child to all who were looking forward to the redemption of Jerusalem. Joseph and Mary marveled at the words of Simeon and Anna. It was affirmation that their innermost faith concerning the heavenly origin of the God-child Jesus was true. When everything required by the Law of Moses had been completed, the Holy Family returned to their home in Nazareth.

Jesus was home-schooled by His mother. From Mary, He learned to read and write and use numbers. Jesus was taught scripture by Mary as she read the scrolls aloud to Him, and she also explained their Jewish traditions. As Jesus grew older, He began working more and more with his foster-father Joseph, learning the craft of carpentry. The child grew and became strong: He was filled with wisdom, and the grace of God was upon Him. And every year the family traveled to Jerusalem at Passover, where they made an offering and worshipped God in the great temple.

Obedience to God and His church and civil authority and, for children, also to their parents, *is the great sign of the Christian.* As a Christian, saying to God "Thy will be done" makes you a spokesperson for Jesus and Mary. Let us meditate on the obedience of Joseph and Mary to temple law. They had God incarnate with them day and night, yet they still observed at great sacrifice the mandates of the priests who prescribed the many Mosaic laws.

Joseph and Mary were poor, as were most people of their day. But it is through humility that God bewilders and mortifies the proud. Which of us could be so humble as to be the parents of the Messiah, and yet keep it hidden in our hearts day after day? But God hides His saints in the stars of the night darkness.

Look at Jesus' amazing humility. He is God, yet He learns scripture from Mary as a spiritually hungry child; and He learns carpentry from Joseph because it is what God and Joseph want. Through humility, Jesus utterly defeated Satan and pride; He exalted only God on High. If we allow pride to rule us, we too can become like Lucifer, raising ourselves up, railing against God.

Now let us little ones visualize Jesus, the Word of God,

as He goes to the temple and reverently worships His Father and their Holy Spirit! Watch as legions of angels praise and adore Jesus. See Jesus as He kneels and prays a long deep prayer to His Father for an abundance of graces for Mary and Joseph. He also prays for the fulfillment of the mission He knows He must one day embark upon. He prays that through His merits *all* men will be saved.

During Jesus' public ministry, He had difficulty teaching the temple high priests and some of the scribes, as they were not always true to the spirit of scripture. Many churches today are being weakened by the tendency to entertain rather than teach, and some are even weakened by immorality. Has your encounter with church people been loving and consoling, or have you been treated harshly, misunderstood, rejected, or gossiped about?

Most people have some negative contact with the church. By this mystery forgive these people who have offended you, and forgive yourself if you have offended others. We all come to the same loving Father who wants us to live together in harmony, especially in our family and in His church.

Eternal Father, I forgive the church, and I forgive my family. I offer you the body, blood, soul, and divinity of your beloved Son, Jesus. Lamb of God, through the Holy Spirit of your eternal law, consecrate me to your Sacred Heart and instill in me the fire of Your Divine Love. Amen; and amen; and amen.

Fifth Joyful Mystery:

Finding of the child Jesus in the Temple

On the third day they came upon him in the temple sitting in the midst of the teachers, listening to them and asking questions (Luke 2:46).

When Jesus was twelve years old, He was taken as is usual for a Jewish family to the temple in Jerusalem for the annual feast of Passover. But after offering prayer and sacrifice, this time his parents "accidentally" left the Temple without Him. Their minds were dimmed by God such that they could go about their business; but that was all. In Jewish custom it was Joseph's responsibility as the head of the family to ensure that Jesus was with them.

After traveling a full day, Joseph and Mary discovered that Jesus was missing from the children's caravan and they returned to Jerusalem. There, Joseph and Mary searched yet another full day before God restored their faculties. They were then able to quickly find Jesus; He was in the temple, listening and teaching. Everyone who heard Jesus was amazed at

His understanding and His answers. When Jesus' parents saw him teaching the most learned priests in the temple, they were astonished.

Jesus' mother said to Him, "Son, why have you treated us like this? Your "father" and I have been anxiously searching for you." They said this not yet realizing that their Heavenly Father had made this happen, blinding them to Jesus' whereabouts. This loss of Jesus for three days had many holy purposes. Jesus helped the priests and elders understand the prophecies of Isaiah concerning Him. Through the intense suffering of Joseph and Mary and their final triumph in finding Jesus, the faith and hope of Jesus' parents were greatly magnified.

Jesus replied to Mary, "Why were you searching for Me. Didn't you know I had to be in my Father's house?" At the time, they did not understand what Jesus was saying. After pondering this mystery, Joseph and Mary understood that Jesus' primary mission was to His Father and that His work of redemption had already begun. They realized that God had given His only begotten Son to the world to save mankind, and that this mission would always be in the forefront of Jesus' mind and life.

Jesus grew in wisdom and stature and in favor with God and man. He became a skillful carpenter under the tutelage of Joseph; it was a skill that would serve Jesus and Mary well in the future. As time went on Joseph became more and more ill, and Mary and Jesus took care of Him for several years. Mary fed Him and gave him fresh clothes and fixed his bed with clean linens. Jesus made furniture to support the family. Then, following months of intense pain, Joseph died and descended to the place of the Patriarchs. He told the patriarchs everything he knew about the Messiah that had first been announced by the innocents whom Herod had killed.

Following Joseph's death, Jesus continued to work as a carpenter to help make a living; and Mary sold clothes she had woven and sewed. During the three years after Joseph's death which was just prior to Jesus' public ministry, Jesus and Mary visited the sick in homes and hospitals whenever and wherever they could, and Jesus discreetly cured the sick and comforted the suffering. They didn't realize until He had left the region that they had been miraculously cured.

Jesus and Mary traveled extensively, and Jesus preached at great length explaining the Messianic prophecies. He told the crowds that the long-awaited Messiah had already been born, without in any way revealing Himself as their Savior. Even when Jesus and Mary weren't fasting, they ate only an evening meal. And every year Jesus and Mary traveled to Jerusalem for the feast of the Passover, where they offered sacrifice and prayer in the temple.

It was a great sacrifice for Jesus and Mary to travel so much to heal and comfort those in need, and to teach the word of God. Do we *"inconvenience"* ourselves by visiting the sick and comforting the suffering? Do we restrain ourselves in the pursuit of pleasure? Our world has advanced so much in human knowledge, but not in spirit; it remains primitive. Let us pray for our world, which has strayed so far from Jesus' teaching. In this mystery, let us be healed of sins against respect, obedience, and charity. Let us adore God simply, as little children.

What a lesson in obedience this mystery is! Jesus went back to Nazareth and was obedient for fifteen years more even though He was already twelve and *He was God Incarnate!* Let us ask ourselves. As parents, are we teaching obedience to our children by word and example?

Jesus wants all young children to view their parents as

God, and always to respect and help them as they grow older. The influx of other cultures may help us in this regard, because many young men and women from nations across the world support their parents in their old age. It is an obligation they assume and carry out in great hardship, even when living in a new country with a different culture.

One of the greatest fears of parents is that a child may be lost and never found, or may leave and never return. Joseph and Mary were filled with fear and anxiety over the loss of Jesus partly because their minds were dimmed. Finally after three sleepless nights, they found the child Jesus in the temple and were greatly relieved; a huge burden was lifted. Have you lost a child to drugs? Vow to fight legalization and use of this great multiform evil! Have you lost a child temporarily or permanently through accident or death? Ask Jesus to heal you of the deep pain you carry in your spirit.

Good and gentle Jesus, before Your face we humbly kneel; and with burning soul we pray and beseech You to fix deep in our hearts lively feelings of faith, hope, and charity. We ask You to strengthen us through suffering. You are our Savior, our light, our life and our companion. Amen; and amen; and amen.

Joyful Reflections of Saints

The Holy Rosary is the storehouse of countless blessings   *-Bl. Alan de la Roche*
Never will anyone who says his Rosary every day be led astray. This is a statement that I would gladly sign with my blood.   *-St. Louis de Montfort*
The saints must be honored as friends of Christ and children and heirs of God. Let us carefully observe the manner of life of all the apostles, martyrs, ascetics, and just men who announced the coming of the Lord. And let us emulate their faith, charity, hope, zeal, life, patience under suffering, and perseverance unto death so that we may also share their crowns of glory.   *-St. John Damascus*
Mary gave to the world the Life that renews all things and she was enriched by God with gifts appropriate to such a role. It is no wonder, then, that the usage prevailed among the holy Fathers whereby they called the mother of God entirely holy and free from all stain of sin, fashioned by the Holy Spirit

into a kind of new substance and new creature. Adorned from the first instant of her conception with the splendors of an entirely unique holiness, the Virgin of Nazareth is, on God's command, greeted by an angel messenger as "full of grace". To the heavenly messenger she replies: "Behold the handmaid of the Lord, be it done to me according to thy word."

-Constitution on the Church, (56)

Enriched from the first instant of her conception with the splendor of an entirely unique holiness, the Virgin of Nazareth is hailed by the heralding angel, by divine command, as 'full of grace' (cf. Lk 1:28). To the heavenly messenger she replies: 'Behold the handmaid of the Lord; be it done to me according to thy word' (Lk 1:38). Thus the daughter of Adam, Mary, consented to the word of God, became the Mother of Jesus. Committing herself wholeheartedly and impeded by no sin to the Lord, to the person and work of her Son, under and with him, serving the mystery of redemption, by the grace of Almighty God.   *-Constitution on the Church, 56*

We can say that the mystery of the redemption took shape beneath the heart of the Virgin of Nazareth when she pronounced her "fiat." From then on, under the special influence of the Holy Spirit, this heart, the heart of both a virgin and a mother, has always followed the work of her Son and has gone out to all those whom Christ has embraced and continues to embrace with inexhaustible love. For that reason her heart must have the inexhaustibility of a mother.

-Pope John Paul II (in his work "Redeemer of Man")

In those days a decree went out from Caesar Augustus that the whole world should be enrolled. This was the first enrollment, when Quirinius was the governor of Syria. So All went to be enrolled, each to his own town. And Joseph too went up from Galilee from the town of Nazareth to Judea, to the city of David that is called Bethlehem, because he was

of the house and family of David, to be enrolled with Mary, his betrothed, who was with child. While they were there, the time came for her to have her child and she gave birth to her firstborn son. She wrapped him in swaddling clothes and laid him in a manger, because there was no room for them in the inn.
-Lk 2:1-7

The angel of the Lord appeared to them and the glory of the Lord shone around them, and they were struck with great fear. The angel said to them, "Do not be afraid; for behold, I proclaim to you good news of great joy that will be for all the people. For today in the city of David a savior has been born for you who is the Messiah and Lord.
-Lk 2:9-11

I turn to you, dear parents, and implore you to imitate the Holy Family of Nazareth.
-St. John Vianney

Remember that the Christian life is one of action; not of speech and daydreams. Let there be few words and many deeds, and let them be done well.
-St. Vincent Pallotti

The proof of love is in the works. Where love exists, it works great things. But when it ceases to act, it ceases to exist.
-Pope St. Gregory the Great

Remember that the Christian life is one of action; not of speech and daydreams. Let there be few words and many deeds, and let them be done well.
-St. Vincent Pallotti

Go forth in peace, for you have followed the good road. Go forth without fear, for he who created you has made you holy, has always protected you, and loves you as a mother. Blessed be you, my God, for having created me.
-St. Clare

Love God, serve God: everything is in that.
-St. Clare of Assisi

He does much in the sight of God who does his best, be it ever so little.
-St. Peter of Alcantara

The first step of humility is unhesitating obedience, which comes naturally to those who cherish Christ above all.

-*St. Benedict (Rule of St. Benedict 5:1-2)*

Remember that you are dust, and unto dust you shall return. Turn away from sin, and be faithful to the Gospel.

-*Formulas used for the imposition of ashes.*

All of us can attain to Christian virtue and holiness, no matter in what condition of life we live and no matter what our life work may be.   -*St. Francis de Sales*

This is the business of our life. By labor and prayer to advance in the grace of God, till we come to that height of perfection in which, with clean hearts, we may behold God.

-*St. Augustine*

During those days Mary set out and traveled to the hill country in haste to a town of Judah, where she entered the house of Zechariah and greeted Elizabeth. When Elizabeth heard Mary's greeting, the infant leaped in her womb, and Elizabeth, filled with the Holy Spirit, cried out in a loud voice and said, "Most blessed are you among women, and blessed is the fruit of your womb. And how does this happen to me, that the mother of my Lord should come to me? For at the moment the sound of your greeting reached my ears, the infant in my womb leaped for joy. Blessed are you who believed that what was spoken to you by the Lord would be fulfilled."   -*Lk 1:39-45*

When the time arrived for Elizabeth to have her child she gave birth to a son. Her neighbors and relatives heard that the Lord had shown his great mercy toward her, and they rejoiced with her. When they came on the eighth day to circumcise the child, they were going to call him Zechariah after his father, but his mother said in reply, "No. He will be called John." But they answered her, "There is no one among your relatives who has this name." So they made signs, asking his father what he wished him to be called. He asked for a tablet and wrote, "John is his name," and all were amazed. Immediately his mouth was opened, his tongue freed, and he spoke blessing God. Then fear came upon all their neighbors, and all these matters were discussed throughout the hill country of Judea. All who heard these things took them to heart, saying, "What, then, will this child be?" For surely the hand of the Lord was with him.   -*Lk 1:57-66*

When Jesus was born in Bethlehem of Judea, in the days of King Herod, behold, magi from the east arrived in Jerusalem, saying, "Where is the new born king of the Jews? We saw his star at its rising and have come to do him homage." When Herod heard this, he was greatly troubled, and all Jerusalem with him. Assembling all the chief priests and the scribes of the people, he inquired of them where the Messiah was to be born. They said to him, "In Bethlehem of Judea, for thus it has been written through the prophet: 'And you Bethlehem, land of Judah, are by no means least among the rulers of Judah; since from you shall come a ruler, who is to shepherd my people Israel.'" Then Herod called the magi secretly and ascertained from them the time of the star's appearance. He sent them to Bethlehem and said, "Go and search diligently for the child. When you have found him, bring me word, that I too may go and do him homage." After their audience with the king, they set out. And behold, the star they had seen at its rising preceded them, until it came and stopped over the place where the child was. They were overjoyed at seeing the star, and on entering the house they saw the child with Mary his mother. They prostrated themselves and did him homage. Then they opened their treasures and offered him gifts of gold, frankincense, and myrrh. And having been warned in a dream not to return to Herod, they departed for their country by another way.   -*Mt. 2:1-12*

That obedience may be complete, it must exist in three things: in execution, by doing promptly, cheerfully and exactly whatever the Superior orders; in will, by willing nothing but what the superior wills; in judgment, by being of the same opinion as the Superior.   *-St. Ignatius Loyola*

A truly obedient man does not discriminate between one thing and another, since his only aim is to execute faithfully whatever may be assigned to him.   *-St. Bernard*

When Herod realized that he had been deceived by the Magi, he became furious. He ordered the massacre of all the boys in Bethlehem and its vicinity two years old and younger, in accordance with the time he had ascertained from the magi. Then was fulfilled what had been said through Jeremiah the prophet: "A voice was heard in Ramah, sobbing and loud lamentation; Rachel weeping for her children, and she would not be consoled, since there were no more."   *-Mt 2:16-18*

Your life consists in drawing nearer to God. To do this, you must endeavor to detach yourself from visible things and remember that in a short time they will be taken from you.   *-Bl. John of Avila*

There is more value in a little study of humility and in a single act of it than in all the knowledge in the world.   *-St. Theresa of Avila*

One just soul can attain pardon for a thousand sinners.   *-St Margaret Mary Alacoque*

Labour without stopping; do all the good works you can while you still have the time.   *-St. John of God*

He who would climb to a lofty height must go by steps, not leaps.   *- Pope St. Gregory the Great*
          (in a letter to St. Augustine of Canterbury)

If we are able to enter the church day and night and implore God to hear our prayers, how careful we should be to hear and grant the petitions of our neighbor in need.

-St. John the Almoner

Now, Master, you may let your servant go in peace, according to your word, for my eyes have seen your salvation, which you prepared in sight of all the peoples, a light for revelation to the Gentiles, and glory for your people Israel. - Simeon at the presentation of Jesus   *-(Lk 2:29-32)*

The highest degree of meekness consists in seeing, serving, honoring, and treating amiably, on occasion, those who are not to our taste, and who show themselves unfriendly, ungrateful, and troublesome to us.   *- St. Francis de Sales*

We must above all show charity to our enemies. By this you may know that a man is a true Christian, if he seeks to do good to those who wish him evil.   *-St. Alphonsus Liguori*

Life well employed consists in a faithful correspondence to grace and a good use of the talents given. There is no other religion than this, and the rule of life is the same for all.

-Blessed Théophane Vénard

If we have obtained the grace of God, none shall prevail against us, but we shall be stronger than all who oppose us.

-St. John Chrysostom

We must also mortify our tongue, by abstaining from words of detraction, abuse, and obscenity. An impure word spoken in jest may prove a scandal to others, and sometimes a word of double meaning, said in a witty way, does more harm than a word openly impure.   *-St. Alphonsus Liguori*

In the first place, the eyes must be mortified. We must abstain from looking at any object that may give occasion to temptation.   *-St. Alphonsus Liguori*

Satisfaction consists in the cutting off of the causes of the sin. Thus, fasting is the proper antidote to lust; prayer to pride, to envy, anger and sloth; alms to covetousness.

-St. Richard of Chichester

Would we wish that our own hidden sins should be divulged? We ought, then, to be silent regarding those of others.   - *St. John Baptist de la Salle*

The spirit flows to you and to all men from the heart of the God-man, Savior of the world, but certainly, no worker was ever more completely and profoundly penetrated by it than the foster father of Jesus, who lived with Him in closest intimacy and community of family life and work. Thus, if you wish to be close to Christ, we again today repeat, "Go to Joseph" (Gn 41:44)   *-Pope Pius XII*

Consider the shortness of time, the length of eternity, and reflect how everything her below comes to an end and passes by. Of what use is it to lean upon that which cannot give support?   *-St. Gerard Majella*

Who is so strong as never to be overcome by temptation, except he who has the grace of the Lord for his helper?
                              -St. Augustine

We ought to respect the image of God in everyone.
                              -Bl. Raphaela Mary

Never utter in your neighbor's absence what you would not say in their presence.   *-St. Mary Magdalen de Pazzi*

It is necessary, too, that we shun the occasions which have been the cause of sin. We must have recourse to fervent prayer, receive frequently and worthily the sacraments. He who does this will be sure to persevere.   *-St. John Vianney*

It is on humble souls that God pours down His fullest light and grace. He teaches them what scholars cannot learn, and mysteries that the wisest cannot solve He can make plain to them.   *-St. Vincent de Paul*

God loves the poor, and consequently He loves those who have an affection for the poor. For when we love anyone very much, we also love his friends.   *-St. Vincent de Paul*

By the effective exercise of only one virtue, a person may attain to the height of all the rest. *-St. Gregory Nazianzen*

If it were given a man to see virtue's reward in the next world, he would occupy his intellect, memory and will in nothing but good works, careless of danger or fatigue.
-St. Catherine of Genoa

Christ said, 'I am the Truth'; he did not say 'I am the custom.' *-St. Toribio*

However great the work that God may achieve by an individual, he must not indulge in self-satisfaction. He ought rather to be all the more humbled, seeing himself merely as a tool which God has made use of. *-St. Vincent de Paul*

Alms are an inheritance and a justice which is due to the poor and which Jesus has levied upon us.
-St. Francis of Assisi

We must give alms. Charity wins souls and draws them to virtue. *-St. Angela Merici*

Run from places of sin as from the plague.
-St. John Climacus

To know whom to avoid is a great means of saving our souls. *-St. Thomas Aquinas*

Take care not to meddle in things which do not concern you, nor even allow them to pass through your mind; for perhaps you will not then be able to fulfill your own task.
-St. John of the Cross

The first step to be taken by one who wishes to follow Christ is, according to Our Lord's own words, that of renouncing himself - that is, his own senses, his own passions, his own will, his own judgement, and all the movements of nature, making to God a sacrifice of all these things, and of all their acts, which are surely sacrifices very acceptable to the

Lord. And we must never grow weary of this; for if anyone having, so to speak, one foot already in Heaven, should abandon this exercise, when the time should come for him to put the other there, he would run much risk of being lost.

-*St. Vincent de Paul*

Idleness begets a life of discontent. It develops self-love, which is the cause of all our miseries, and renders us unworthy to receive the favors of divine love.   -*St. Ignatius Loyola*

Let it be assured that to do no wrong is really superhuman and belongs to God alone.   -*St. Gregory Nazianzen*

She could do more because she loved more.

-*St. Gregory the Great (speaking of Scholastica)*

Charity is the form, mover, mother and root of all the virtues.   -*St. Thomas Aquinas*

If I were worthy of such a favor from my God, I would ask that he grant me this one miracle: that by His grace He would make of me a good man.   -*St. Ansga*

Fly from bad companions as from the bite of a poisonous snake. If you keep good companions, I can assure you that you will one day rejoice with the blessed in Heaven; whereas if you keep with those who are bad, you will become bad yourself, and you will be in danger of losing your soul.

-*St. John Bosco*

Charity is the sweet and holy bond which links the soul with its Creator: it binds God with man and man with God.

-*St. Catherine of Sienna*

If according to times and needs you should be obliged to make fresh rules and change current things, do it with prudence and good advice.   -*St. Angela Merici*

This is a virgin's birthday; let us follow the example of her chastity. It is a martyr's birthday; let us offer sacrifices; it is the birthday of holy Agnes: let men be filled with wonder, little ones with hope, married woman with awe, and the unmarried with emulation. It seems to me that this child, holy beyond her years and courageous beyond human nature, received the name of Agnes (Greek: pure) not as an earthly designation but as a revelation from God of what she was to be.   *-St. Augustine*

The soul who is in love with God is a gentle, humble and patient soul.   *-St. John of the Cross*

Christ, the Master of humility, manifests His Truth only to the humble and hides Himself from the proud.

-St. Vincent Ferrer

Humility is so precious that it obtains the things that are to high to be taught. It attains and possesses what words do not attain.   *-Bl. John Ruysbroeck*

The devil only tempts those souls that wish to abandon sin and those that are in a state of grace. The others belong to him: he has no need to tempt them.   *-St. John Vianney*

The principal trap which the devil sets for the young people is idleness. This is the fatal source of all evil. *-St. John Bosco*

He who prays most receives most. *-St. Alphonsus Liguori*

Humility is the safeguard of chastity. In the matter of purity, there is no greater danger than not fearing danger.

-St. Philip Neri

The first end I propose in our daily work is to do the will of God; secondly, to do it in the manner he wills it; and thirdly to do it because it is his will.   *-St. Elizabeth Ann Seton*

Purity is the special reward of being humble.

-St. John Bosco

The bread which you use is the bread of the hungry; the garment hanging in your wardrobe is the garment of him who is naked; the shoes you do not wear are the shoes of the one who is barefoot; the acts of charity that you do not perform are so many injustices that you commit. *-St. Basil*

God must be loved first, in order that one's neighbor, too, may be loved in God. *-St. Bernard*

For the LORD sets a father in honor over his children; a mother's authority he confirms over her sons. He who honors his father atones for sins; he stores up riches who reveres his mother. He who honors his father is gladdened by children, and when he prays he is heard. He who reveres his father will live a long life; he obeys the LORD who brings comfort to his mother. *-Sirach 3:2-6*

If you have too much to do, with God's help you will find time to do it all. *-St. Peter Canisius*

The greatest honor God can do a soul is not to give it much, but to ask much of it. *-St. Therese of Lisieux*

It is important that you choose your career with care, so that you may really follow the vocation that God has destined for you. No day should pass without some prayer to this end. Often repeat with St. Paul: "Lord, what will you have me do?" *-St. John Bosco*

You must ask God to give you power to fight against the sin of pride which is your greatest enemy - the root of all that is evil, and the failure of all that is good. For God resists the proud. *-St. Vincent de Paul*

Pride makes us forgetful of our eternal interests. It causes us to neglect totally the care of our soul. *-St. John Baptist de la Salle*

Do not fear that the occupations imposed by obedience will draw you away from union with God: for when they are performed for His glory they have, instead, great power to unite us closely to Him. For how can those things separate us from God, which unite our will to his? The whole mistake arises from the failure to distinguish between being drawn away from God, and being drawn away from the sweetness found in the interior perception of God. It is true that in occupation this sweetness is not always enjoyed (though it is sometimes in the highest degree); but in depriving ourselves of this for the love of God, we gain instead of losing, while we leave the weak for the strong. While to quit or abandon our work to unite ourselves to God by prayer, reading, or recollection, by solitude and contemplation, would be to withdraw from God and unite ourselves to ourselves and to our own self-love. - *St. Francis de Sales*

The Luminous Mysteries

First Luminous Mystery

The Baptism of Jesus

And when Jesus was baptized,...the heavens were opened and He saw the Spirit of God descending like a dove, and alighting on Him, and lo, a voice from heaven, saying "this is My beloved Son," with whom I am well pleased (Mathew 3:16-17).

Early one bright sunny morning, the time had arrived for Jesus to leave the warmth and comfort of His Mother's lovely little home to go out into the world. The dew sparkled as the sun peaked through the rustling leaves. After Jesus had walked a short distance, He looked back and waved to His smiling Mother; how He had enjoyed her love and her home: the restful shade under the tree, the garden, the blooming flowers, the birds, bees, butterflies. But Jesus knew that His Heavenly Father was persistently calling Him ever so gently, and He was *eager* to please His Father. He heard God's Spirit whispering in the soft breeze, caressing Him, leading Him where He knew not.

Mary had been His gentle, caring mother for thirty years. What great love bonded them we cannot even imagine. Jesus told Mary that He would always let her know where he would be, and would meet her whenever possible. But Jesus, the Word, was on a mission that day as He marched forward with the torch of holiness and truth and light to bring peace and healing to the entire world.

Thus did Jesus depart to minister to the chosen people and to evangelize at every opportunity, a responsibility He would formally receive in baptism. He was determined to follow the will of His Father wherever this great adventure might lead. Jesus had heard of John baptizing at the river Jordan, and inspired, He swiftly journeyed to see that great event.

Many people were there that day at the river Jordan, witnessing the baptism of all who repented. They saw Jesus in his clean white tunic go into the river too. They watched as He was immersed in the waters of the Jordan by John, and they saw the love flow from His Father, as their Holy Spirit descended upon Jesus like a dove. In His divine-human condition Jesus *is* without sin. But in a single holy act, Jesus established baptism as a new sacramental covenant by which we would be cleansed of sin and receive the gifts of the Holy Spirit; and if we were an adult in grave sin, we would regain son-ship and inheritance with Our Heavenly Father.

Many of us have witnessed the baptism of a beautiful little baby. Baptism is an inspirational event by which a new citizen of heaven is created. In the soul of the baptized, Our Father and His Son are confirmed as one in union with their Holy Spirit. Baptism is the holocaust of Christ, created by Him to infuse us with grace and virtue and gift. The baptized becomes a new creature of God, and the fire of the Holy Spirit overflows and proclaims to the whole world, *"This is my newly beloved!"*

Picture yourself as a little girl or boy reliving your own baptism. See the light of the Easter candle radiantly beam off your new white dress or suit; see the reflections in the baptismal font. Hear the words of illumination, "Receive the light of Christ. We anoint you with the oil of salvation in the name of Christ our Savior... You have become a new creation..." Now feel the fresh warm water trickling over your head three times, hear the purifying words, "I baptize you in the name of the Father, and of the Son, and of the Holy Spirit...

Feel the warm towel lovingly caress your head. The priest asks, "What do you ask of God's church?" You answer, "The grace of Christ and eternal life." You feel the Holy Spirit of God descend upon you, warm you, enlighten you. You glow inside and out, and you boldly proclaim, "Father, I was made by you, I belong to You; Lord, give me the inheritance promised of old..."

We were clothed in Jesus' innocence when we were baptized! A friend told me that Jesus once said to him, "Stop sinning so you are clean when I take you to my Father." Thus, we face a formidable task, a daunting challenge; to become, and to remain, pure and holy. We can do this through prayer and the sacraments, particularly the sacraments of Reconciliation and Eucharist. Are you availing your soul of these indescribable grace-filled opportunities *as intensely and frequently as you can?*

Most of us are already baptized, so how can we achieve even greater sanctity? Our soul was initially created by God; thus it is perfect, created in God's image and likeness. Everyone is born to a woman, an imperfect creature; and thus our body is imperfect. At the time we were baptized as babies, we received many graces and new responsibilities.

If we are baptized as an adult having *chosen God out of love,* in addition to all the other graces and new responsibilities we also attain new greater perfections of body and soul. As a baby who has grown into an adult, we can still attain these new perfections of charity by being reborn in the spirit, putting on the new man who is born of the fruit of the great sacrifice of Jesus crucified! And new perfections of charity make us clearer charitable images of our Heavenly Father.

Jesus, in the name of your Eternal Father forgive my sins, and through the special grace of the Holy Spirit cleanse me anew that I may be as pure and grace-filled as I was at my baptism. I wish to be reborn in your Spirit, Lord, that I may become more like your Father. Help me to fulfill my mission to evangelize in your most blessed name, Jesus of Nazareth. Amen.

Second Luminous Mystery

The Wedding at Cana

His mother said to the servants, "Do whatever He tells you." ... Jesus said to them, "Fill the jars with water." And they filled them up to the brim (John 2:5-7).

As a little child, Jesus' parents were like God to him, providing whatever He needed. As Jesus grew to boyhood, He was deeply touched by the warm, caring ways manifested by His Mother and foster-father towards him and each other. As a young man Jesus learned about human love from Mary and Joseph. Jesus had before Him an example of greatest love and service, as both tried to do all that was humanly possible to bring happiness to each other, to the family. They ate together, laughed together, and dreamed together.

Our ideas of man and woman come primarily from our parents. Jesus had before Him Joseph and Mary. What a bright clear image Jesus had of what a man and a woman united for life should be like. As Jesus grew into a man, this was His way with others too; what great love He showed to all of the people He met. Jesus had begun His public ministry before the wedding of Cana, and with His newly chosen apostles He had rejoined His mother there. Jesus went to the wedding because the communal joining of a man and woman was something very dear, very sacred in the Heart of Jesus. Once there, He felt compelled to bless and to save the day for His hosts.

At the Jewish wedding in Cana, six jars of water were used for the ceremonial washing of hands. Looking into the future, Jesus intended this be replaced by the sacrament of Reconciliation. At the wedding Jesus miraculously turned water into wine. At the Last Supper, Jesus blessed bread and wine and it became His body and blood, foreshadowing the sacrament of the Holy Eucharist. Through the establishment of these sacraments, Jesus kept His promise to remain with us to the very end.

In the mystery of the wedding of Cana, Jesus established Matrimony as a holy sacrament uniting male and female. Their two families are joined in love. In the marriage covenant, husband and wife become one in spirit and are to love and believe firmly in each another. Husband loves wife, wife loves husband, and from their love a child proceeds.

The family is, in a sense, similar to the Blessed Trinity. In the Trinity, each person loves and admires the other; Father loves Son, Son loves Father, and from an outpouring of their reciprocal love *is* the Holy Spirit of God. A family is to live and love like the Trinity. When a family lives with the Triune God paramount in their lives, there is love and admiration and unity and peace.

Is your family like the Holy Family in spirit? Does your family, as one, peacefully embrace God and His Church? When was the last time you attended a wedding? Do you not remember it well? Jesus, Mary, and Joseph's presence is so powerful at wedding masses! Remember the pretty white flowers, the flickering white candles in crystal sparkling holders, the bride's beautiful white wedding dress, the colorful dresses of the bridesmaids! How happy and kind everyone is, love is everywhere.

You see the priest query the couple about their love, their commitment. The priest is ready to seal their new covenant with golden rings of fire. The man solemnly swears his everlasting love and allegiance to his bride, and then you see the radiance of the bride as she beams back her love and commitment. The priest proclaims to the whole community of believers, *"I now pronounce you man and wife,"* and the two are blissfully joined in love and purpose and spirit.

Marriages begin so beautifully, but sometimes troubles arise years later. For this reason many people today request prayers for their family. When a family is hurting it might be because of a child in trouble. The parents are in deep pain for their children. Sometimes it is the marriage itself, as it can be less than satisfying. Jesus said, "Come to me, all you who labor and are burdened, and I will give you rest (Matthew 11:28)."

Today we see disorder in society as some engage in same-sex partnerships. It is a form of unbelief and hatred against God. Let us follow the lead of our Supreme Pontiff in opposition to all ungodly activities. Lord, we ask You to rid our society of all ungodly acts, of all unbelief in your holy laws and traditions and institutions.

Jesus, touch my heart that it may become aflame with love for You and my spouse. Lord, you touched the marriage at Cana in a most special way; heal my marriage of

any negativity. Make my spouse one with me in love and purpose and spirit. As in a blissful marriage, Jesus, let the flame of Your Spirit lift me to your heavenly embrace of eternal happiness. Amen.

Third Luminous Mystery

Proclaiming the Kingdom

"And preach as you go forth, saying, 'The Kingdom is heaven is at hand.' Heal the sick, raise the dead, cleanse lepers, cast out demons. You received without pay, give without pay (Matthew 10:7-8).

Jesus commanded His followers to go forth to heal the sick and share the Gospel. The early Church spread rapidly because of dedication to Christ and to *healing,* which is simply "an answer to prayer." Today Jesus calls us to pray with people who are sick. It can be spiritual sickness, emotional, psychological, relational or physical illness.

Jesus wants His followers to boldly go forth and pray for healing, and to evangelize the unbelievers. "Ask, and you shall receive." Unto every believer is granted the grace to preach the gospel, however humbly. It is a greater miracle to convert an unbeliever than to heal the body, for to do so is to bring the "dead" back to life.

The "kingdom of heaven" on earth is the Christ-life bestowed by Jesus. The gift of life through extraordinary Eucharistic grace is unavailable anywhere but in the Apostolic Church of Jesus Christ. The sacraments originally given by Christ to His apostles and disciples continue to be bestowed upon us by our Church through our priests to this day.

In Baptism we become heirs of heaven, and thus we are united to God in son-ship. The Sacrament of Confirmation empowers us to pray deeply in the Holy Spirit, to evangelize, and to perform great works of mercy. The sacrament of Reconciliation is our wonderful opportunity for deep inner healing, especially when it is joined to our intention of complete forgiveness of ourself and of others. If we are to be forgiven by Our Father, we too must forgive; we should never let the sun set on our wrath.

The Eucharist is rarely spoken of as a healing sacrament, but it is the greatest of all healing opportunities as the Great Healer Jesus Himself comes right within our body and soul. He comes right inside of us. That is as close as He will be to us until we see Him unveiled in heaven, at which time we are in Him as well. In the Eucharist we are evangelized directly by Jesus. This is a necessary prerequisite for our attempts at evangelization of others.

Through the sacraments we are all given increased gifts and graces by the Holy Spirit, and we are to use them all to glorify God in His supreme majesty. Observing the Law of God, obtaining Grace, receiving the Sacraments, and using Sacramentals increases our capacity to perform holy and just actions. It also protects us from the attacks of the evil one.

Has anyone ever spoken so lovingly of people as Jesus! "If anyone gives even a cup of cold water to one of these little ones because he is my disciple...he will certainly not lose his reward...Come to me, all you who are weary and burdened, and I will give you rest…learn from me, for I am gentle and humble of heart, and you will find rest for your souls. For my yoke is easy and my burden is light." There is no doubt, Jesus loves more than all creatures of all time put together!

In reflecting on the third luminous mystery, you can see Jesus standing there high on the mountainside, smiling, tall and handsome. Clothed in white, Jesus is a dazzling figure in the bright warm sunshine. He looks around the vast crowd and caresses the little children with His sapphire blue eyes. He moves slowly to a gentle slope and stands amidst lush grass and wildflowers and a couple of large rocks. Watch as the King of heaven and earth turns to the crowd to give them the good news.

There is a hush among the crowd. Jesus raises His head and loudly proclaims, "The Kingdom of Heaven is at hand." The gentle breeze animates flowers and grasses and trees. In the distance you see trees loaded with fruit. Winged creatures melodiously sing lullabies from dawn to dusk, praising their creator. In the distance, a herd of sheep grazes. Bees and butterflies scurry busily from flower to flower. All eagerly serve their loving creator in their own humble way.

This begets a quiet calm, an unusual peace. Heaven truly touches earth. The Holy Spirit is in Jesus and He begins speaking with great wisdom of His love for his most beloved creature, man. "Exult, you who are thirsty! Exult, you who are hungry! Exult, you who are afflicted!…Exult!…It is no longer so. I give you homes, wealth, paternity, fatherland, heaven! Follow me, exult in my love, for I am Savior, Redeemer; I am the light and the life!"

Jesus stops for a moment, raises His head and arms, and prays to His Father. Then, eagerly, He meanders through the crowd healing the sick, comforting the suffering. Suddenly,

Jesus straightens to His full height; He turns and searches the crowd. And His gaze comes to rest directly on you. His powerful clear blue eyes peer into yours. Jesus smiles warmly. Then slowly, ever so softly Jesus says lovingly, *"My dear friend, I came for you!"*

I thank You, dear Jesus, for saving me and for loving me. You are the pure One; I, the sinner; yet you remain faithfully with me always. You cast your healing, consoling eyes of divine mercy upon me day and night to warm and strengthen my soul at every moment of my life. Amen.

Fourth Luminous Mystery

The Transfiguration

As He was praying, the appearance of His countenance was altered and His raiment become dazzling white. And a voice came out of the cloud saying, "This is My Son, My chosen; listen to Him (Luke 9:29, 35)!"

Jesus calls upon each of us to be transformed by His Grace. He desires to be within each of us, His followers, so that we may constantly encounter Him in one another. In the tabernacle, Jesus is with us at all times. But through the Sacraments, Jesus gives us His own love power for our healing and growth. We return this love to God when we offer Jesus' body, blood, soul, and divinity to His Eternal Father.

We strive to move from the flesh into the Spirit. We yield ourselves to God to allow His Holy Spirit to possess us in the sense of leading us, talking through us, and spiritually working in and through us. We saw that so clearly in the life of Mother Theresa; she allowed herself to be filled with the Holy Spirit. People of every race and creed were touched by her very simple words and writings because they were saturated with the Holy Spirit. We can be the same as Mother Teresa, and we can do the same wonderful works of mercy.

We too can be transformed by the Light of the World, by the Light of the Transfiguration, by the Holy Spirit of Jesus. Let us dwell for a moment on the Transfiguration. Light accompanies the spirit; it is its companion. How marvelous it must have been to see Jesus radiant in all His glory, our God Incarnate humbly speaking to Moses and Elijah. Since the time of the Transfiguration, only a few like Sister Kowalska of Poland have seen the luminous Risen Christ with colored streams of light gloriously emanating from His five most precious wounds. For such is Jesus, the Ocean of Mercy, the light of the world.

You too can see the Transfiguration through your spirit! Gaze now upon this most spectacular event. See the apostles roused by a brilliance surpassing many suns; watch the great light erase every shadow. Jesus stands on a cloud of vapor, shining with an intense light. See Our Lord's eyes beaming, His cloak sparkling, the bright light of the Spirit radiating from His body. See Jesus look upward, enraptured, ecstatic as the intense light of heaven opens.

Two small lights descend to earth, one becoming a man of incandescent light and the other a man colored as the flame of the sun. Listen as Moses and Elijah reverently converse with their God incarnate. Jesus talks about His forthcoming death, His resurrection. Suddenly a cloud of unimaginably brilliant light envelops Jesus, and the powerful harmonious voice of the Father thunders through the heavens, "This is my beloved Son, in whom I am well pleased. Listen to Him!"

In this same light did Jesus enter the Kingdom of the Heavenly Jerusalem forty days after His death, the brilliant light of the Transfigured Christ pouring forth His pure and eternal innocence. Light streamed from His hands and feet, and from the wound in His side. For us, the Transfiguration is all over now. Elijah and Moses stream back towards heaven as two lights, and then disappear in the vast expanse of creation. The cloud before you melts away.

Picture yourself standing there, just you and the apostles with Jesus. Jesus turns towards you, and He looks above you towards heaven and prays to His Father. He prays for you and for all of the living and dead, and for all people yet to be born. Then He lowers His head and looks deep into your eyes, and stretches forth His arms to you. Jesus says quietly, *"See, friend, it is true, I love you."* Jesus' voice drops even more. He resolutely and solemnly says, *"Yes, it is true. I love you so much that I will eagerly die for you."*

Many saints died proving their inestimable love for Jesus. Let us be filled from the rivers of wisdom and mercy that flow unceasingly from the heart of the Divine Mercy. Let us go to Jesus, the tree of life, who sprouts leaves and flowers and indescribable fruits for all those who love Him. We too can live and die for Jesus; *we can live in charity and die to the world through the Eucharist, and we can reach out in love to the very Holy Spirit of our God!*

Lord Jesus , we thank you for showing your divinity to the disciples of the early church. Through your transfiguration you manifested a new path to heaven itself. Illuminate our minds that we may always see you as our most loving friend, Jesus, even in times of heartache and trouble. Amen.

Fifth Luminous Mystery

Institution of the Eucharist

And He took bread, and when He had given thanks He broke it and gave it to them, saying, "This is My body which is given for you." ...And likewise the cup after supper, saying, "This cup which is poured out for you is the new covenant in My blood (Luke 22:19-20)."

Jesus said, "Remain in me and I will remain in you." How can this happen? Normal food changes into our own body and blood. But the Eucharist slowly changes us more and more into a holy being like Christ. We remain in Him when we remain in a state of grace. In so doing, Jesus remains in us as well. We are so privileged. The four beings at the throne of God cannot receive Jesus in the Holy Eucharist, nor can the twenty-four elders, nor the Cherubim and Seraphim and saints and angels; only we have the great joy and blessing to receive the Lord God of Hosts into our body and into our heart.

A great saint once said that there is one thing that God cannot do, and that is to give us more than He has already given us, because He has given us *Himself* in all His love and glory and majesty in the Eucharist. The Eucharist is our most vital spiritual food! St. Rose of Viterbo said, "Prayer reveals to souls... It fills them with light, strength and consolation; and it gives them a foretaste of the calm bliss of our heavenly home." Perseverance in Holy Communion will bring great healing and blessings from the Eucharistic Jesus. Receive the Holy Eucharist worthily as frequently as possible; it is our greatest prayer.

Mary was the flour ground by the millstone most deserving of the bread of life. Jesus was the grain that died to produce infinite Eucharistic blessings. His Spirit is the compendium of the love of His Father and their Spirit. The Eucharist is the love of God, the heavenly banquet prepared for mankind. The Eucharist is the Last Supper before the great messianic "wedding supper" to come in the New Heavenly Jerusalem.

Let us rejoice and be glad and give Him glory! For the wedding feast of the Lamb has come, and His bride has made herself ready. Fine linen, bright and clean, was given her to wear. ...Blessed are those who are invited to the wedding supper of the Lamb! But let us be prepared, for many are called *but* few are chosen.

Picture yourself at mass in your own parish church. You came early, as does Our Blessed Mother. Watch Mary pray for each person, tenderly prepare each heart, sanctify and enlighten and heal. You listen as Old Testament scripture is proclaimed, you hear Jeremiah and Elijah and Isaiah prepare the Way for the coming of the Messiah. Then the Gospel is proclaimed. See Jesus preach the "good news" as he prepares sinners for the coming of the Kingdom. Walk with Him as He teaches and prays and heals.

Then, His mission nearly accomplished, Jesus prepares His greatest gift to man. Visualize Jesus in a large upstairs room with a long wood table in the midst. There is a basin of water and a large white towel. Watch the ceremonial cleansing of feet. Then watch Our Lord bless bread and wine, changing it into His body and blood. Angels adore! You have just "seen" the very first mass.

Now take yourself back to mass at your own church. The priest prays over the water and wine, and then he issues the *great command.* Jesus, humble, ever obedient to His Word, leaves His heavenly throne and becomes a prisoner of the bread and wine. Totally focused on Jesus, you walk towards the altar and come before the priest.

You bow to Jesus in the Eucharist, and partake of the heavenly manna. You are warmed all over, a new peace engulfs you; you feel light, bright and happy. You have become one with the Light of the World, one with your Heavenly King. Once again you are intimately united in mystical love to your Lord and Savior, Jesus Christ. Once again Jesus is in you as your Healer and Teacher.

Let us reflect more on the wonder that is the Eucharist. Since God's "all" is the greatest gift we can receive, should we not avail ourselves of it as reverently and frequently as possible? Jesus suffers much when the Eucharist is casually or infrequently received. After we have received the Eucharist, should we not as a congregation thank Jesus for a few minutes? We thank other people longer for far smaller gifts; let us eagerly thank Jesus for *His infinite gift*!

We all expect to go to heaven and many of us want to bypass purgatory, but are our expectations too high? If we attend mass and receive the Eucharist as frequently and reverently as we can, there is a much greater chance that we will go straight to heaven! Let us pray.

Lord Jesus, we cannot thank You sufficiently for remembering us down through the ages with the Bread of Eternal Life. We firmly believe in Your real presence under the species of bread and wine. Thus, in our holy reception of this sacrament, we believe that we receive within us the one triune God who loved us from time immemorial. Lord, You promise us everlasting happiness in heaven. I promise that I will do my very best to receive the Holy Eucharist as frequently and worthily as I can. Thank you, Jesus, for giving us your most precious gift, *Yourself!* Amen.

Luminous Reflections of Saints

As he was walking by the Sea of Galilee, he saw two brothers, Simon, who is called Peter, and his brother, Andrew, casting a net into the sea; they were fishermen. He said to them, "Come after me, and I will make you fishers of men." At once they left their nets and followed him.   *-Mt 4:18-20*

He walked along a little farther and saw James, the son of Zebedee, and his brother John. They too were in a boat mending their nets. Then he called them. So they left their father Zebedee in the boat along with the hired men and followed him.   *-Mk 1:19-20*

Philip found Nathaniel and told him, "We have found the one about whom Moses wrote in the law, and also the prophets, Jesus, son of Joseph, from Nazareth." But Nathaniel said to him, "Can anything good come from Nazareth?" Philip said to him, "Come and see." Jesus saw Nathaniel coming toward him and said of him, "Here is a true Israelite. There is no duplicity in him." Nathaniel said to him, "How do you know me?" Jesus answered and said to hi, "Before Philip called you, I saw you under the fig tree." Nathaniel answered him, "Rabbi, you are the Son of God; you are the King of Israel." *-Jn 1:45-50*

When Jesus went into the region of Caesarea Philippi he asked his disciples, "Who do people say that the Son of Man is?" They relied, "Some say John the Baptist, others Elijah, still others Jeremiah or one of the prophets. He said to them, "But who do you say that I am?" Simon Peter said in reply, "You are the Messiah, the Son of the Living God." Jesus said in reply, "Blessed are you Simon son of Jonah. For flesh and blood has not revealed this to you, but my heavenly Father, and So I say to you, you are Peter, and on this rock I will build my church, and the gates of the netherworld shall not prevail against it. *-Mt 16:13-18*

And many of the Jews had come to Martha and Mary to comfort them about their brother. When Martha heard that Jesus was coming, she went to meet him: but Mary sat at home. Martha said to Jesus, "Lord, if you had been her, my brother would not have died. Even now I know that whatever you ask of God, God will give you." Jesus said to her, "Your brother will rise." Martha said to him, "I know he will rise, in the resurrection on the last day." Jesus told her, "I am the resurrection and the life; whoever believes in me, even if he dies, will live, and everyone who lives and believes in me will never die. Do you believe this?" She said to him, "Yes, Lord. I have come to believe that you are the Messiah, the Son of God, the one who is coming into the world. *-Jn 11:19-27*

Thomas said to him, "Master, we do not know where you are going; how can we know the way?" Jesus said to him, "I am the way and the truth and the life. No one comes to the Father except through me. If you know me, then you will also know my Father. From now on you do know him and have seen him." Philip said to him, "Master show us the Father, and that will be enough for us." Jesus said to him, "Have I been with you for so long a time and you still do not know me, Philip? Whoever has seen me has seen the Father. How can you say, 'Show us the Father'? Do you not believe that I am in the Father and the Father is in me? The words that I speak to you I do not speak on my own. The Father who dwells in me is doing his works. Believe me that I am in the Father and the Father is in me, or else, believe because of the works themselves. Amen, amen, I say to you, whoever believes in me will do the greater ones than these, because I am going to the Father. And whatever you ask in my name, I will do, so that the Father may be glorified in the Son. If you ask anything of me in my name, I will do it.   *-Jn 14:5-14*

When they had finished breakfast, Jesus said to Simon Peter, "Simon, son of John, do you love me more than these?" He said to him, "Yes, Lord, you now that I love you." He said to him, "Feed my lambs." He then said to him a second time, "Simon son of John, do you love me?" He said to him, "Yes Lord, you know that I love you." He said to him, "Tend my sheep." He said to him a third time, "Simon, son of John, do you love me?" Peter was distressed that he said to him a third time "Do you love me?" and he said to him, "Lord, you know everything; you know that I love you." Jesus said to him, "Feed my sheep. Amen, amen, I say to you, when you were younger, you used to dress yourself and go where you wanted; but when you grow old, you will stretch out your hands, and someone else will dress you and lead you where you do not want to go." He said this signifying by what kind of death he would glorify God. And when he had said this, he said to him, "Follow me."   *-Jn 21:15-19*

Through the paschal mystery we have been buried with Christ in baptism, so that we may rise with him to a new life.

Now that we have completed our lenten observance, let us renew the promises we made in baptism when we rejected Satan and all his works, and promised to serve God faithfully in His holy Catholic Church.

-Taken from prayers on Easter Sunday
in the Sacramentary

He presented himself alive to them by many proofs after he had suffered, appearing to them during forty days and speaking about the kingdom of God. While meeting with them, he enjoined them not to depart from Jerusalem, but to wait for the "promise of the Father about which you have heard me speak; for John baptized with water, but in a few days you will be baptized with the Holy Spirit."   *-Acts 1:3-5*

It is necessary, too, that we shun the occasions which have been the cause of sin. We must have recourse to fervent prayer, receive frequently and worthily the sacraments. He who does this will be sure to persevere.   *-St. John Vianney*

It is on humble souls that God pours down His fullest light and grace. He teaches them what scholars cannot learn, and mysteries that the wisest cannot solve He can make plain to them.   *-St. Vincent de Paul*

Holy Communion is the shortest and safest way to Heaven. There are others: Innocence, for instance, but that is for little children. Penance, but we are afraid of it. Generous endurance of the trials of life, but when they come we weep and ask to be spared. The surest, easiest, shortest way is by the Eucharist.   *-Pope St. Pius X*

In all He did from the Incarnation to the Cross, the end Jesus Christ had in mind was the gift of the Eucharist, his personal and corporal union with each Christian through Communion. He saw in It the means of communicating to us all the treasures of His Passion, all the virtues of His Sacred

Humanity, and all the merits of His Life.

-St. Peter Julian Eymard

Christ, like a skillful physician, understands the weakness of men. He loves to teach the ignorant and the erring he turns again to his own true way. He is easily found by those who live by faith and to those of pure eye and holy heart, who desire to knock at the door, he opens immediately.

-St. Hyppolytus (Treatise on Christ and Antichrist)

It often happens that we pray God to deliver us from some dangerous temptation, and yet God does not hear us but permits the temptation to continue troubling us. In such a case, let us understand that God permits even this for our greater good. When a soul in temptation recommends itself to God, and by His aid resists, O how it then advances in perfection.

-St. Alphonsus Liguori

This is our daily Bread; take It daily, that It may profit thee daily. Live, as to deserve to receive It daily.

-St. Augustine

Whereas in the Lord's Prayer, we are bidden to ask for 'our daily bread,' the Holy Fathers of the Church all but unanimously teach that by these words must be understood, not so much that material bread which is the support of the body, as the Eucharistic bread, which ought to be our daily food.

-Pope St. Pius X

In this dark vale of tears, I wish solely to feed upon this secret manna, this delicious substance.   *-St. Cajetan*

After six days Jesus took Peter, James and John and led them up a high mountain apart by themselves. And he was transfigured before them, and his clothes became dazzling white, such as no fuller on earth could bleach them. Then Elijah appeared to them along with Moses, and they were conversing with Jesus. Then Peter said to Jesus in reply,

"Rabbi, it is good that we are here! Let us make three tents: one for you, one for Moses and one for Elijah." He hardly knew what to say, they were so terrified. Then a cloud came, casting a shadow over them; then from the cloud came a voice, "This is my beloved Son. Listen to him." Suddenly, looking around, they no longer saw anyone but Jesus alone with them.

-Mk 9:2-8

Receive Lord, all my liberty, my memory, my understanding and my whole will. You have given me all that I have, all that I am, and I surrender all to your divine will, that you dispose of me. Give me only your love and your grace. With this I am rich enough, and I have no more to ask.

-St. Ignatius Loyola

He is generous even to exhaustion; and what is most wonderful is, that He gives Himself thus entirely, not once only, but every day, if we wish it. Every fresh Communion is a new gift which Jesus Christ makes of Himself.

-St. Ignatius Loyola

Let us adore His power, exhausting itself in this act of love.　　　　　　　　　　　　　　*-St. Peter Julian Eymard*

Jesus is the teacher of holiness. I go to Him because I want Him to teach me how to become a saint. Of what use to me is all I learn In school if I do not become holy?

-St. Francis de Sales

Before you receive Jesus Christ, you should remove from your heart all worldly attachments which you know to be displeasing to Him.　　　　　　　　　　*-St. Augustine*

A soul can do nothing that is more pleasing to God than to communicate in a state of grace.　　*-St. Alphonsus Liguori*

If we wish to make any progress in the service of God we must begin every day of our life with new eagerness. We must keep ourselves in the presence of God as much as possible

and have no other view or end in all our actions but the divine
honor. *-St. Charles Borromeo*

I can no longer live without Jesus. How soon shall I receive Him again? *-St. Maria Goretti*

The state of marriage is one that requires more virtue and constancy than any other: it is a perpetual exercise of mortification. *-St. Francis de Sales*

All the wealth in the world cannot be compared with the happiness of living together happily united.
-Bl. Margaret d'Youville

No tongue can express the greatness of the love which Jesus Christ bears to our souls. He did not wish that between Him and His servants there should be any other pledge than Himself, to keep alive the remembrance of Him.
-St. Peter of Alcantara

The Blessed Sacrament is the first and supreme object of our worship. We must preserve in the depths of our heats a constant and uninterrupted, profound adoration of this precious pledge of Divine Love. *-St. Mary Euphrasia Pelletier*

With supernatural intuition, Blessed Josemaria untiringly preached the universal call to holiness and apostolate. Christ calls everyone to become holy in the realities of everyday life. Hence work too is a means of personal holiness and apostolate, when it is done in union with Jesus Christ.
-Pope John Paul II at the beatification of
Josemaria Escriva

Go to Jesus. He loves you and is waiting for you to give you many graces. He is on the altar surrounded by angles adoring and praying. Let them make some room for you and join them in doing what they do. *-St. Mary Joseph Rossello*

The saints are like the stars. In his providence Christ conceals them in a hidden place that they may not shine before others when they might wish to do so. Yet they are always ready to exchange the quiet of contemplation for the works of mercy as soon as they perceive in their heart the invitation of Christ. *-St. Anthony of Padua*

It is only by sacrifice and suffering, offered as penance, that you will be able, by the grace of God, to convert sinners. *-St. John Vianney*

O God, seeing you are so infinitely lovable, why have you given us but one heart to love you, and this so little and so narrow? *-St. Philip Neri*

You ought to make every effort to free yourselves even from venial sin, and to do what is most perfect. *-St. Theresa* of Avila.

In this dark vale of tears, I wish solely to feed upon this secret manna, this delicious substance. *-St. Cajetan*

Do not imitate those who deceive themselves by saying: "I will sin and then go to confession." How do you know that you will have time to make your confession? Is it not madness to wound oneself, in the hope that a doctor will be found who will heal the wound? *-St. John Bosco*

Repentance is the renewal of Baptism and a contract with God for a second life. *-St. John Climacus*

He loves, He hopes, He waits. If He came down on our altars on certain days only, some sinner, on being moved to repentance, might have to look for Him, and not finding Him, might have to wait. Our Lord prefers to wait Himself for the sinner for years rather than keep him waiting one instant. *-St. Peter Julian Eymard*

After confession, thank Almighty God for the pardon which you have received, and renew your good resolution never more to offend Him, and to avoid all occasions of sin; and pray to Jesus and Mary for perseverance. *-St. Alphonsus Liguori*

Nothing restrains anger, curbs pride, heals the wound of malice, bridles self-indulgence, quenches the passions, checks avarice and puts unclean thoughts to flight, as does the name of Jesus.   *-St. Bernard*

It is not only among us, who are marked with the name of Christ, that the dignity of faith is great; all the business of the world, even of those outside the Church, is accomplished by faith. By faith, marriage laws join in union persons who were strangers to one another. By faith, agriculture is sustained; for a man does not endure the toil involved unless he believes he will reap a harvest. By faith, seafaring men, entrusting themselves to a tiny wooden craft, exchange the solid element of the land for the unstable motion of the waves. Not only among us does this hold true but also, as I have said, among those outside the fold. For though they do not accept the Scriptures but advance certain doctrines of their own, yet even these they receive on faith.

-St. Cyril of Jerusalem (Catechesis V)

Christ shield me this day:
Christ with me,
Christ before me,
Christ behind me,
Christ in me,
Christ beneath me,
Christ above me,
Christ on my right,
Christ on my left,
Christ when I lie down,
Christ when I arise,
Christ in the heart of every person who thinks of me,
Christ in every eye that sees me,
Christ in the ear that hears me

-St. Patrick (from his breastplate)

The Most Blessed Sacrament is Christ made visible. The poor sick person is Christ again made visible.

-*St. Gerard Majella*

If you commit any sin, repent of it at once and resolve to amend. If it is a grievous sin, confess it as soon as possible.

-*St. Alphonsus Liguori*

Hence we must say that for the knowledge of any truth whatsoever man needs divine help, that the intellect may be moved by God to its act. But he does not need a new light added to his natural light, in order to know the truth in all things, but only in some that surpasses his natural knowledge.

-*St. Thomas Aquinas*

I remind you to stir into flame the gift of God that you have through the imposition of my hands. For God did not give us a spirit of cowardice but rather of power and love and self-control. So do not be ashamed of your testimony to our Lord, nor of me, a prisoner for his sake; but bear your share of the hardship for the gospel with the strength that comes from God.

-*St. Paul in his second letter to Timothy (2 Tim 1:6-8)*

Visits to the Blessed Sacrament are powerful and indispensable means of overcoming attacks of the devil. Make frequent visits to Jesus in the Blessed Sacrament and the devil will be powerless against you.

-*St. John Bosco*

Go to your adoration as one would go to Heaven, to the divine banquet. Tell yourself, "in four hours, in two hours, in one hour our Lord will give me an audience of grace and love. He has invited me; He is waiting for me; He is longing for me."

-*St. Peter Julian Eymard*

God's mercy is like an unleashed torrent; it bears away all hearts in its flood.

-*St. John Vianney*

Throughout the world, the Second Sunday of Easter will receive the name Divine Mercy Sunday, a perennial invitation to the Christian world to face, with confidence in divine benevolence, the difficulties and trials that humankind will experience in years to come.

-Decree of the Congregation for Divine Worship issued on 23 May, 2000 instituting Divine Mercy Sunday

"Love one another. As I have loved you, so you must love one another." *-Jesus (John 13:34)*

God in his omnipotence could not give more, in His wisdom He knew not how to give more, in His riches He had not more to give, than the Eucharist. *-St. Augustine*

THE SORROWFUL MYSTERIES

First Sorrowful Mystery

The Agony in the Garden

In his anguish he prayed with all the greater intensity, and his sweat became like drops of blood falling to the ground. Then he rose from prayer and came to his disciples, only to find them asleep, exhausted with grief (Luke 22:44-45).

It is evening and the dew is falling heavily. That very evening Jesus had washed the feet of the apostles and instituted the sacrament of Eucharist. Jesus knows that the temple priests seek His death, and He knows that Judas will betray Him. Jesus slowly climbs the Mount of Olives in deep thought; He leaves Peter and his companions to go off and pray by Himself. Jesus sees the lights of Jerusalem below, but He turns His back to it and finds a large rock. He kneels and prays a deep, fervent prayer to His Father. He prays that man may be saved from Satan, the world, the flesh, and from his own weakness.

Jesus sees things that upset Him greatly, He begins to

weep; agitated, He unfolds His arms, and tears stream down His face. Jesus prays; He is in terrible distress. Finally after what seems hours, He grabs His mantle, dries His tears, and goes back to Peter.

But Peter and his companions had lit a fire and are basking in its crackling warmth, sound asleep, aided by tiredness and food and grief! This same thing happens a second time; they all fall asleep and Jesus again awakens them pleading with them to pray. But this time as Jesus returns to the large rock and begins praying, a bright light appears, resting a little above Jesus' head. It grows brighter and brighter. It is an angel who has come to console Jesus. The angel names, one by one, all of the people Jesus will save through His passion and death. It is a majestic sight, the King of Love bathed in angelic light, comforted by heaven itself. His mission complete, the light of the angel slowly fades away.

Jesus goes back to Peter and commands him and the other two to awaken, telling them that *"Satan never sleeps."* He declares, "My time has come." They get up and walk hurriedly to the other apostles, gather them, and are just about to leave. But they see lights, wavering from side to side, approach them. All of a sudden a large band of priests and Temple guards break into the open with torches, ropes, and clubs in hand. Judas Iscariot leads them; smiling, he kisses Jesus on the cheek. Jesus asks Judas Iscariot, "Why have you come for me? Are you betraying me with a kiss? Put away your swords and clubs. I am not a threat; I have always been with you."

Peter interprets this as resistance by Jesus, so he bravely flashes his sword and swings, and a soldier, rope upraised, jumps aside. The wild swing of Peter's sword nearly cut his ear off. But Jesus reprimands Peter for his lack of understanding and acceptance of His Father's will. He tells Peter that if

He wanted it, a legion of five thousand angels would be here to defend Him. At this, Jesus' followers desert him. Thus was the night of Jesus' betrayal by Judas Iscariot for a mere thirty pieces of silver; thus did He treat His friend and close companion of three years. Jesus is tied and led away.

Jesus was tried in the temple court in the very same temple in which He and Mary had prayed at the feast of Passover each year. His temple judges were lead by the wicked Chief Priest Annas and High Priest Caiaphas. They had been told in advance of Jesus' whereabouts by Judas, and they had charged the Temple guards with the arrest of Jesus.

We must wonder if Jesus would be safe even in our world today, or whether He would suffer a similar fate, with everybody abandoning Him. More importantly, we must wonder if we ourselves are spiritually strong. Would we resist the subtle forces of the world that attack and destroy good whenever and wherever possible, or would we just stand by and watch.

As God, Jesus knew that He was destined for the ignominious death of the cross, and that He would be betrayed by His "friend" and companion, Judas. But Jesus and Mary harbored no ill will towards Judas, who always seemed on the verge of death in the spirit. Rather, they prayed for him and tried to get him to change his ways to the very end. Jesus showed an undying active love, even for His betrayer. Are we steady in our love for our parents, spouses, children, friends, and those in need? Do we pray and offer up our suffering as we ought? Even for our enemies?

Visualize Jesus agonizing in the garden over the mental suffering that He would have to undergo. The divine part of his person was willing to go forward, but His human nature pulled back at all of the suffering He knew was coming. He dreaded the passion and crucifixion that he had seen in His spirit, but He was eager to suffer it for the sake of Redemption. Jesus suffered the agony of internal conflicts knowing His mother was to see Him tortured to death. When a loved one is hurt in some way, we too may suffer the intense torture of not being able to do anything about it. Often we become totally helpless, as were Jesus and Mary. Jesus felt crushing pain in His heart, but He chose to follow His Father's will. When have you suffered the same turmoil? Often we want to do what God calls us to do, but we humanly rebel. Has this happened to you? Do you need to be healed of a particular incident? Ask Jesus for this healing now! Jesus is willing to heal this agony in our heart through this First Sorrowful Mystery. Invite Jesus back to that devastating moment and ask Him to set you free. Hasn't He come to us "to set the captives free?"

Jesus, I agonize as I meditate upon your passion, as You knew not all people would be saved. I realize that it was the suffering your mother and friends would have to endure that grieved you so greatly. Jesus, loving redeemer, have mercy on us when we are in agony. Console us, and send us Your Holy Spirit Comforter to help us through our suffering. Amen.

Second Sorrowful Mystery:

The Scourging of Jesus

Pilate's next move was to take Jesus and have him scourged (John 19:1).

The Chief Priests had turned Jesus over to Pontius Pilate, and Pilate had sent Him to King Herod for judgment. A Roman Centurion now returns from Herod's palace and tells Pilate that Herod has sent Jesus back, and he reports what transpired. Pilate ponders his next move, and then remembers an old custom. He turns to the Judeans and says, "I questioned Jesus and found no fault in Him, and neither did Herod. Thus, Herod has sent Him back to us. But in order to make you happy, I will give you Barrabas, and I will order that your Christ be given forty lashes."

But the crowd is moved to great fury, yelling more loudly than ever, "No, death to Him! Death to the Nazarene!" Somewhat unsure of himself Pilate says, "I will give him forty lashes, is that not enough?" Pilate and the Judeans are well aware that scourging is far more painful than whipping. So

Pilate feels this is a terrible punishment, and that it should certainly satisfy this bloodthirsty fanatical crowd. But the frenzied mob screams all the more, No! Crucify Him! Crucify Him!

Pilate is now more afraid of the mob than he is of the wrath of any God. He tells the Judeans, "The matter is over, I have decided," and he retires to an interior room, very angry with the Jews. Jesus is led off by Praetorian guards through a hall to a courtyard to be scourged. Many people died under Roman scourging, and Jesus had probably seen this during his lifetime. Jesus knew he had to suffer this terrible torture, but He willingly went forth. There was nothing, humanly speaking, that He could do about it.

They wait for mercenaries to come to do the scourging, and finally they arrive. Jesus meekly takes off his tunic at their command, and His hands are tied tightly to a large iron ring in the ceiling by a soldier standing on a stool. Two burly, unkempt men move in, laughing, brandishing scourges. One goes in front of the Lord, one behind him. They begin to beat Jesus like a drum, rhythmically. They skillfully use the scourges, handles with steel balls attached to the ends of new leather thongs.

The first sight of fresh blood spurs them into a frenzy, and they strike harder, faster, more furiously, iron balls and leather pummeling and cutting. Jesus begins to slump into semi-consciousness; His full weight hangs from the iron ring. Jesus' skin is criss-crossed with thong cuts. Already swollen from the rope used to drag Him to the house of Annas, Jesus' midriff swells the more and His raw skin burns like hot coals. He is cut, bruised black and blue, bleeding from head to foot. The first piece of skin flies off the shoulder of Jesus, cut clean by the sharp edges of the thongs. Now the fury of the attack increases, the flogging quickens. Raw flesh is struck, blood gushes.

This continues for what seems hours, though it is *only* for part of an hour. By then the thoroughly fatigued mercenaries are ordered to break off the attack as Jesus looks like He is dead. Jesus is untied; He crumbles to the hard marble floor. He is not dead, but He is a mass of cuts and bruises, raw flesh, and bright fresh blood spurting here and there. A soldier kicks Him to see if He is alive; He moves a little.

Slowly Jesus regains His senses, He tries to push Himself up, tries to rise to His knees. After struggling for some time, Jesus finally is able to stand. He painfully puts His tunic back on. It becomes red with blood and yellow-white from sticky fluids emanating from His body. The soldiers tie Jesus' wrists again. There is no rest for Jesus; He is dragged, half dead, to an outside courtyard. Jesus is the picture of the servant described in the Bible, Isaiah's prophetic "suffering servant."

Do we suffer and pray for souls in union with Our Lord and Mary? Jesus was turned over for punishment by the corrupt Roman leader Pontius Pilate, who knew from his spies that Jesus was innocent. Pilate yielded to the pressure of the world even though scourging an innocent victim was immoral and he knew it. He had the power to set Jesus free, but fear of endangering his own power and position took precedence over his moral duty.

We are all called to live in order, justice, and love. Jesus suffered scourging to save sinners that would otherwise be lost. Jesus and Mary continue to suffer and pray to this very day for this same purpose because more is constantly being created in the way of sin. Let us pray for the conversion of the world and to delay the coming of judgment until its appointed time!

Will we unite our sufferings to Jesus and Mary and patiently bear with the pains and inconveniences of life? What is the greatest pain in your life right now? Offer it up in union with the sufferings of Jesus, for immolation is perfect love. It is redemptive if we share it with Jesus. Ask Jesus for the grace to offer up those pains that you must continue to live with. Offer all of your suffering to Jesus, and know that many people will receive graces of conversion or an increase in holiness as you suffer with Jesus.

Pray especially for your spouse and children. God dresses all our wounds, and only the scars are left to remind us of our victorious suffering. One day they will shine in the luminous light of the New Jerusalem!

Jesus, help us to contemplate Your suffering more frequently and intensely. This day we pray that You will unite our suffering to Yours for the conversion of sinners and unbelievers, and for release of the most needy souls in Purgatory. We promise that we will meditate more deeply upon the most sorrowful mysteries of the Rosary. Amen.

Third Sorrowful Mystery:

The Crowning with Thorns

They stripped off his clothes and wrapped him in a scarlet military cloak. Weaving a crown out of thorns they fixed it on his head, and stuck a reed in his right hand (Matthew 27:28-29).

Following the scourging, one of the soldiers guarding Jesus says, "*Now what* shall we do with this man? I am bored." "I know," says the other; "The Judeans wanted a king, so let us give them one!" The soldier hastily retreats to the outer courtyard where he cuts several branches off a hawthorn bush. Others join in his effort, cutting the leaves off with a stout knife so that only thorns remain. With some difficulty they weave a few of the branches together forming a circle or "crown," with multiple thorny cords interlaced in the front and ends bulging with knots at the back.

The sharp thorny crown is placed over Jesus' head, but it drops down to his neck. Angrily, clumsily, the brigands tear the circle of thorns off Him because it's too large, but in doing so they scratch Jesus' face, nearly tearing His eyes out. They also scratch and cut their own hands but, cursing, work the more furiously. They make the crown smaller, try to force it onto Jesus' head, but it still won't stay on; it doesn't "stick." Now it's *too small!*

They remove the crown a third time, each time tearing off more of Jesus' hair. The rogues enlarge the "crown" a little, and this does the trick, now it's *just right*. They press it on hard and step back, happily admiring their handiwork. Jesus puts His head down, He appears stoic in the face of their derision, though He is suffering terribly.

Now the soldier that thought up the idea of the crown of thorns begins to make fun of Jesus, saying how nice he looks bedecked with a crown of precious jewels. But he devisively states that the crown isn't sufficient to make Him a king. He yells to another soldier of lesser rank, "Get Jesus a scepter and a royal purple robe!" The soldier searches, but all he can find is a cane that they make Jesus hold in His right hand, and a red rag they throw over His shoulder. This is alright; it's what they really wanted anyway, to humiliate Jesus more.

One of the soldiers, laughing, grabs the stick out of Jesus' hand and starts beating him furiously over the head with it. The others burst into laughter and applause! It drives the thorns deeper while cutting the skin, because the crown moves as it is struck. Jesus says nothing, He just lifts His head and looks at all of them so kindly and sadly that it would break the heart of anyone that is human. They continue this treatment until they get the order of a ranking officer to bring the Prisoner back to Pilate.

Jesus, crown on His head and red rag around His shoulder, is taken to Pilate. Pilate looks sympathetically at the badly wounded Man. He contrasts Jesus with the arrogant mob, and says, "Here He is, here is the man I punished, now let Him go!" But they yell that they want to see Him better. Jesus is brought forward and displayed to His people. The crowd has become huge now, well over a thousand. Jesus gazes at them, He searches for friendly faces. How many are there? Only a few, and tears form in Jesus' eyes and begin to stream down his face. Pilate says, "Here He is, here is the Man you wanted punished. Is this not enough torture for your King?"

Crowning with thorns was not a prescribed or preordained Roman or Jewish punishment, but was invented solely by man's gift of imagination. Satan played no part in the crowning. Picture Jesus before you, crowned with thorns. Blood oozes from His head where the thorns have torn His flesh. Jesus writhes in agony, the thorns not allowing Him to relieve His tiredness or rest His head for even a moment.

How is it that we, His most favored creatures, could fall so low as to treat our loving innocent benefactor so horribly? It is because of sin, that age-old evil. Sin weakens us spiritually, makes perversion pleasurable. Let us pray and act against cruelty and injustice whenever possible. When we are treated unfairly, let us become sacrificial lambs like Jesus to lighten the burden of sin upon our patient heavenly Father's shoulders.

Let us pray for forgiveness of those sins committed by any part of our head. In particular, let us consecrate our lips to the Lord. Let us never gossip, for we must keep our lips sanctified on account of what proceeded from them in the Person of Jesus. Do not be deceived in anything and do not speak falsehoods, for by so doing we falsify His Word; and *God will not be derided*. Let us consecrate also our ears and mind and heart, joining them to Jesus' Holy Spirit.

In this mystery of the crowning with thorns, we petition

by Jesus' great sufferings that we be set free from head pain or given the grace of bearing it in a redemptive way. Most of us have suffered from head pain that prevents us from functioning properly and cheerfully. So many need healing of the head from falls, eye or ear pain, sinus irritations, aneurisms, strokes, tumors and cancer of the brain.

Ask Jesus to heal your physical and mental pain. But if we must bear it, let us offer it up for the conversion or healing of a family member or friend, even an enemy. Now let us pray for the conversion of our family members most in need.

Lord Jesus, touch those in my family that need healing of the head. Eternal Father, I offer up the body, blood, soul, and divinity of Your beloved Son Jesus in reparation for all of the sins I have committed with my eyes, ears, and tongue. Father, I petition You for forgiveness for myself and for my whole family.

Fourth Sorrowful Mystery:

Carrying of the Cross

...Carrying the cross by himself, He went out to what is called the Place of the Skull (in Hebrew, Golgotha (John 19:17).

The board with the inscription, "Jesus Nazarene, King of the Jews," has been tied to a rope and the noose is placed over Jesus' head. Jesus starts out on His way to Calvary; the cross bounces hard on the steps as they go down stairs to the street. Jesus begins to pant; He is short of breath almost as soon as He begins to exert Himself. As Jesus reaches the street, the waiting mob sees that the rope around Jesus' neck rotates the thorn crown as the board swings from side to side. They applaud with approval, and laugh and are reinvigorated by the sight of more blood.

A paved barren road lies ahead. As Jesus weakens and loses His breath, He falls to both knees, and the cross falls to the ground on top of Him. The thud is heard over the noise of the crowd, crushing the thorns deep into His neck. Jesus

76

struggles to get up, the full weight of the cross making it almost impossible, but the soldiers help him up and then spur Him on. An accompanying woman offers Jesus a cool white linen cloth taken from a repository, and with her aid Jesus wipes His perspiration. Jesus thanks all of the women and tells them this injustice will be severely punished. He tells them, "Weep not for me. But for your sins and those of your towns." The order to proceed is given, and with some help Jesus lifts the cross to His bloody shoulder and continues.

A group of women accompanied by some shepherds are standing in the middle of the road, and they are the first to see Jesus coming. They alert mother Mary and John. The procession moves along. They get closer, and Mary sees her beaten, broken Son for the first time. She gasps in shock. Mary is white as death, and she is barely able to stand. The exhausted Jesus looks ever so lovingly at His mother, His cheeks sunk, lips bleeding, pale face distorted and swollen from blows to His head.

The observant Roman Commander Longinus spots a man driving a cart. He orders him over, asks his name and is told "Simon of Cyrene." Longinus tersely commands Simon, "Take his cross and carry it for him!" Simon turns and walks slowly towards Jesus. Jesus is so bent from pain and exhaustion that he seems to be dying on His feet. His eyes are half closed, his breathing labored.

Even the hardened Roman soldiers are moved to pity by the scene that has unfolded before their eyes. They become pensive. They think of their own mothers, and for a short time they are lost in their memories. They become like little boys as, for this brief moment in time, they fall prey to their own emotions. How different life was when they were little, how dear it was. How innocent they were then. But they had grown into young men and, with very little knowledge of the world, had been trained in the cruelties of warfare and sent to faraway places to fight. They fondly remembered saying their final farewells to their own loving mothers.

Now picture Jesus in this most sorrowful mystery. He is a dying man carrying the tremendous weight of the heavy bouncing cross that slivers His flesh and presses the thorns deeper into His head. The fact that the soldiers forced Simon of Cyrene to help Jesus shows that our Lord was in an extremely helpless condition.

We too may be experiencing great pain in our lives. It could be family trouble, our spouse, or one of our children in trouble of some sort. It could be caused by alcoholism, drugs, gambling or by financial problems. Perhaps our pain is due to the disease of pride or foolishness; it may be caused by a debilitating physical disease, and maybe by a relative or close friend dying. There is such a feeling of isolation and helplessness!

When have you been in utter need and no one would volunteer to help you, not even a relative or friend whom you thought you could depend on? Forgive that person who disappointed you so greatly. It may be someone that you trusted completely. Ask Jesus to give you the grace to forgive, and to be healed of that painful memory. We can be of help to others in need. We can pray for them, visit them, share our financial blessings, or help victims get into programs of self-help. We can be their earthly saviors in union with Jesus!

Who are the people that *you* refused to help in some way? Perhaps you disappointed someone when they came to you in pain seeking your support. Did you find an excuse to turn them away? Have you just "pretended" to be a friend? Jesus is most merciful towards involuntary faults, but He is inexorable towards calculated impenitent acts of hypocrisy. Forgive yourself, and if you can, ask those whom you should have helped for forgiveness. Jesus *wants to set you free of this sorrow* through this mystery.

Beloved Jesus, carry my crosses with me that I may aid in the redemption of sinners. You were tired carrying your own heavy cross. Give me the strength, especially when I am most exhausted, to help others in need, that I may work for Your greater honor and glory. Amen.

Fifth Sorrowful Mystery:

The Crucifixion

Jesus uttered a loud cry and said, "Father, into your hands I commend my spirit." After he said this, he expired (Luke 23:46).

Jesus has carried His cross to Golgatha in great pain. He cannot hide His mass of sores, dark coagulated blood and scabs, contusions, and fresh bright blood. His neck is bleeding, and His back, shoulders, and chest are criss-crossed with ugly open gashes. The first drops of blood fall on the white veil given Jesus by His mother that had become wet with her tears, and bright red stains appear. Jesus has so much pain in His internal organs that he cannot stand upright, so He remains bent in utmost pain like a very old man.

Jesus' head feels like it is encompassed in a vise of nails; it stings and burns as do His eyes, and sharp pain shoots through His head every time his "crown" moves or is bumped, particularly sore is His forehead and the back of His neck. Jesus' jaw is dislocated to the right. His chest, arms and legs are criss-crossed with red stripes and black and blue bruises. His knees are bloody, and one kneecap is severely torn. His toes ache and bleed from rocks on the road and from repeated stumbling.

It is Jesus' turn to be fastened to the cross. Meekly He lies down on the cross when ordered. He lays His head down exactly where instructed. He stretches out His arms and legs as directed. Two executioners squat on His chest, sitting back to back. Jesus cannot move, He can hardly breathe. Jesus lies there, unmoving, waiting for the first stroke of the hammer on the large spike held to His right wrist.

The third executioner takes Jesus' arm, pulls it tight, and holds it there with both hands. The fourth executioner checks to see that Jesus' wrist is directly over the hole and, when satisfied, he raises his hammer and strikes the huge square spike. Jesus gives a sharp cry as pain floods through His arm, the spike crushing nerves and flesh in His wrist. The right wrist is now securely nailed against the dark wood of the cross.

The executioner moves to the other side. The man with the spike places it in the middle of Jesus' hand, and pounds it. This pain is far worse, but Jesus only moans and groans at the penetration. Tears mix with blood and run across His face onto the cross, down onto the ground. Jesus' face looks bizzare as it is a dirty black with red and white stripes where blood and sweat flow.

The executioner moves to the feet. The spike punctures a large hole through both feet and they are securely fastened, both pinned to the block of wood. Mary, too, watches all of this most intensely. She feels Jesus' immense pain, and she bends lower at each pound of the hammer. Her flesh is slowly being crushed, her agony is excruciating.

And Jesus is really weakening fast now. He lets His head

hang forward from time to time to rest it, as the thorns prevent Him from laying it back against the cross. Suddenly, Jesus gathers all His strength, and He speaks, "Woman, behold your son. Son, behold your mother." Jesus' breathing is more and more labored; His heart beats irregularly, spasmodically; his hoarse voice emits sounds that come from collapsing tissues. Jesus raises His head to His Father and shouts in a loud voice, "Eloi, Eloi, lamma sabactini." His face has taken on the final look of death. Jesus falls forward more and more, His knees bend more sharply, His weakness increases.

But Jesus summons all His strength and shouts one last time as only a desperate man can, "Father, into your hands I commit my spirit!" There is one last spasm, and Jesus hangs motionless, no longer breathing. Suddenly, there is a final convulsion and the very last utterance of Jesus; He cries loudly, "Mo…" It is the first syllable of mother, the very last cry narrated in the gospel. Jesus' head falls heavily to His chest, He does not stir. *Jesus is dead!*

We all know the story of how Jesus died a slow, painful death on the cross. We also know the sad story of those who deserted Him, leaving His mother and John beneath the cross with only a few men and women in the background. Death is the greatest of all traumas according to psychologists. Most people have a deep fear of dying, not knowing what to expect at the moment of passage to another world. There is nothing for us to do but to be open and accept death.

Unfortunately, few today see death as part of the great mercy of God; but it is only the unjust who die in grave unrepentant sin who would want to come back into the world. Have our lives been pleasing to Our Father? Will Jesus smile and hug us and cover us with His robe of light and life before He takes us to His Father? It will be much easier for us when we are on our deathbed if we have done our best to follow Jesus!

Once again, let us picture Jesus being nailed to the cross. He knows the torture His mother feels as the spikes penetrate his hands and feet. Mary was granted her request to feel all of the suffering of Jesus, all of His physical pain and mental anguish. She knew, as did her Son, that for so many Jesus' great suffering would not save them. Jesus and Mary knew that so many would never leave their sinful ways; and this greatly magnified their pain. Yet, Mary had to let go of her Son, it was the will of her Heavenly Father; it was for the redemption of the world!

It is very difficult for us, too, to let go of our loved ones. Cast all of your suffering upon the Lord who takes care of you. Ask Jesus to heal you of the trauma of the one death in your life that has caused you the most pain. He wants to set you free of the subconscious hurts that attended the death of a loved one.

Also ask for the grace of a happy death for yourself and your family. Seek to be free of the powerful fear of death that prevents us from living peacefully. We will be even more relaxed and joyful when the Lord heals us of this strong emotion of fear. Jesus' death is bearing much fruit in our lives as we are healed from the blocks of His great love.

Finally, let us reflect on Jesus' infinite love. He was crucified solely for our benefit, not for the angels, not for the ancient ones. What an extraordinary, loving event; our very creator God returning the human family to His Holy Family by dying for us! We are so precious that He would do anything to return us to His friendship! We are so precious to Our Father that He would pay the ultimate price for our salvation; He would sacrifice His only Son. How willing are we to sacrifice in comparison to God, the Infinite Charity? Let us try even harder to love Jesus as He loves us!

Heavenly Father and Holy Spirit, we know that you too suffered with Jesus in His passion as you are one God; the Trinity of inseparable, holy and innocent love. Forgive us for our sins, we humbly implore You. Beloved Jesus, You are the eternal expiator. Would that I had offered my life in place of yours. Like Mary, I long to comfort You in Your agony. Jesus, help me to thank You for Your caring love and healing graces; for saving me from eternal darkness; and for restoring my Father's inheritance so that I may live forever with You in heaven. Amen.

Sorrowful Reflections of Saints

He was chosen by the eternal Father as the trustworthy guardian and protector of his greatest treasures, namely, his divine Son and Mary, Joseph's spouse. He carried out this vocation with complete fidelity until at last God called him, saying 'Good and faithful servant, enter into the joy of your Lord.'   *-St. Bernadine of Siena*

This very moment I may, if I desire, become the friend of God.   *-St. Augustine*

Whatever did not fit in with my plan did lie within the plan of God. I have an ever deeper and firmer belief that nothing is merely an accident when seen in the light of God, that my whole life down to the smallest details has been marked out for me in the plan of Divine Providence and has a completely coherent meaning in God's all-seeing eyes. And so I am beginning to rejoice in the light of glory wherein this meaning will be unveiled to me.

-St. Teresa Benedicta of the Cross

A man who governs his passions is master of the world. We must either command them, or be enslaved by them. It is better to be a hammer than an anvil. *-St. Dominic*

Our Lord gives to souls of prayer a deep understanding of Himself. He never deceives them. *-St. Peter Julian Eymard*

The poor stretch out the hand, but God receives what is offered. *-St. Peter Chrysologus*

You cannot please both God and the world at the same time, They are utterly opposed to each other in their thoughts, their desires, and their actions. *-St. John Vianney*

I have often been sorry for having spoken, but never for holding my tongue.
-St. Arsenius (one of the forty four maxims)

The Lord measures our perfection neither by the multitude nor the magnitude of our deeds, but by the manner in which we perform them. *-St. John of the Cross*

Our actions have a tongue of their own; they have an eloquence of their own, even when the tongue is silent. For deeds prove the lover more than words. *-St. Cyril of Jerusalem*

No sacrifice is more acceptable to God than zeal for souls.
-St. Gregory the Great

It is better to be the child of God than king of the whole world. *-St. Aloysius Gonzaga*

Know that the experience of pain is something so noble and precious that the Divine Word, who enjoyed the abundant riches of Paradise, yet, because He was not clothed with this ornament of sorrow, came down from Heaven to seek it upon the earth. *-St. Mary Magdalen de' Pazzi*

Under the influence of fear, we bear the Cross of Christ with patience. Under the more inspiring influence of hope, we carry the Cross with a firm and valiant heart. But under the consuming power of love, we embrace the Cross with ardour. *-St. Bernard*

He who trusts himself is lost. He who trusts in God can do all things. *-St. Alphonsus Liguori*

O Sacred Heart of Jesus! I fly to Thee, I unite myself with Thee, I enclose myself to Thee! Receive this, my call for help, O my Saviour, as a sign of my horror of all within me contrary to Thy Holy Love. Let me rather die a thousand times than consent! Be Thou my Strength, O God: defend me, protect me. I am thine, and desire forever to be Thine!
-St. Margaret Mary Alocoque

I make myself a leper with the lepers, to gain all for Jesus Christ. *-Bl. Damien Joseph de Veuster*

An evil thought defiles the soul when it is deliberate and consented to. Our Lord placed evil thoughts at the head of all crimes, because they are their principle and source.
-St. John Baptist de la Salle

Then one of the Twelve, who was called Judas Iscariot, went to the chief priests and said, "What are you willing to give me if I hand him over to you?" They paid him thirty pieces of silver, and from that time on he looked for an opportunity to hand him over. *- Mt 26:14-16*

It was now about noon and darkness came over the whole land until three in the afternoon because of an eclipse of the sun. Then the veil of the temple was torn down the middle. Jesus cried out in a loud voice, "Father, into your hands I commend my spirit"; and when he had said this he breathed his last. The centurion who witnessed what had happened glorified God and said, "This man was innocent beyond doubt." When all the people who had gathered for this spectacle saw what had happened, they returned home beating their breasts; but all his acquaintances stood at a distance, including the women who had followed him from Galilee and saw these events.   *-Lk 24:44-49*

After this, Joseph of Arimathea, secretly a disciple of Jesus for fear of the Jews, asked Pilate if he could remove the body of Jesus. And Pilate permitted it. So he came and took his body. Nicodemus, the one who had first come to him at night, also came bringing a mixture of myrrh and aloes weighing about one hundred pounds. They took the body of Jesus and bound it with burial cloths along wit the spices, according to the Jewish burial custom.   *- Jn 19:38-40*

For five weeks of Lent we have been preparing, by works of charity and self-sacrifice, for the celebration of our Lord's paschal mystery. Today we come together to begin this solemn celebration in union with the whole Church throughout the world. Christ entered in triumph into his own city, to complete his work as our Messiah: to suffer, to die, and to rise again. Let us remember with devotion this entry which began his saving work and follow him with a lively faith. United with him in his suffering on the cross, may we share his resurrection and new life.

-Taken from Palm Sunday in the Sacramentary

The crosses with which our path through life is strewn associate us with Jesus in the mystery of His crucifixion.

-St. John Eudes

But since all your satisfactions and penances are too small and deficient to atone for so many sins, unite them to those of you Savior Jesus lifted upon the Cross. Receive his Divine Blood as it flows from His wounds, and offer It up to appease Divine justice. Unite your reparation to that of the most Blessed Virgin at the foot of the Cross and from the love of Jesus for His Mother, you will obtain everything.

-St. Peter Julian Eymard

We should strive to keep our hearts open to the sufferings and wretchedness of other people, and pray continually that God may grant us that spirit of compassion which is truly the spirit of God.   -*St. Vincent de Paul*

What does it cost us to say: "My God, help me! Have mercy on me!" Is there anything easier than this? And this little will suffice to save us if we be diligent in doing it.
                                              -*St. Alphonsus Liguroi*

O Priest! You are not yourself because you are God. You are not of yourself because you are the servant and minister of Christ. You are not you own because you are the spouse of the Church. You are not yourself because you are the mediator between God an man. You are not from yourself because you are nothing. What then are you? Nothing and everything. O Priest! Take care lest what was said to Christ on the cross be said to you: "He saved others, himself he cannot save!"
                                              -*St. Norbert*

He who faithfully prays to God for the necessaries of this life is both mercifully heard, and mercifully not heard. For the physician knows better than the sick man what is good for the disease.   -*St. Augustine*

Do not condemn, even with your eyes, for they are often deceived.   -*St. John Climacus*

Take heed not to foster thy own judgment, for, without doubt, it will inebriate thee; as there is no difference between an intoxicated man and one full of his own opinion, and one is no more capable of reasoning than the other.
                                              -*St. Francis de Sales*

Take the holy crucifix in your hands, kiss its wounds with great love, and ask Him to preach you a sermon. Listen to the thorns, the nails, and that Divine Blood say to you Oh! What a sermon.   -*St. Paul of the Cross*

God is full of compassion, and never fails those who are afflicted and despised, if they trust in Him alone.

- St. Teresa of Avila

When you feel the assaults of passion and anger, then is the time to be silent as Jesus was silent in the midst of His ignominies and sufferings.

-St. Paul of the Cross

I trust in Christ that he will enable me to undergo, in defense of his cause, the sharpest tortures you can inflict on my weak body.

-St. Theophanes

We must show charity towards the sick, who are in greater need of help. Let us take them some small gift if they are poor, or, at least, let us go and wait on them and comfort them.

-St. Alphonsus Liguori

The patient and humble endurance of the Cross - whatever nature it may be - is the highest work we have to do.

-Bl. Katherine Drexel

All our religion is but a false religion, and all our virtues are mere illusions and we ourselves are only hypocrites in the sight of God, if we have not that universal charity for everyone - for the good, and for the bad, for the poor and for the rich, and for all those who do us harm as much as those who do us good.

-St. John Vianney

Stand fast, therefore, in this conduct and follow the example of the Lord, 'firm and unchangeable in faith, lovers of the brotherhood, loving each other, united in truth,' helping each other with the mildness of the Lord, despising no man.

-St. Polycarp (Letter to Philippians)

The body dies when the soul departs; but the soul dies when God departs.

-St. Augustine

I will not live an instant that I do not live in love. Whoever loves does all things without suffering, or, suffering, loves his suffering.

-St. Augustine

Go down into the abyss, you evil appetites! I will drown you lest I myself be drowned! -*St. Jerome*

The only reason for my being killed is that I have taught the doctrine of Christ. I thank God it is for this reason that I die. I believe that I am telling the truth before I die. I know you believe me and I want to say to you all once again: Ask Christ to help you become happy. I obey Christ. After Christ's example, I forgive my persecutors. I do not hate them. I ask God to have pity on all, and I hope my blood will fall on my fellow men as a fruitful rain. -St. Paul Miki

Jesus Christ, Lord of all things! You see my heart, you know my desires. Possess all that I am - you alone. I am your sheep; make me worthy to overcome the devil. -*St. Agatha*

That hope is deceitful which hopes to be saved amid the occasions of sin. -*St. Augustine*

As God recognized each of us before we were born, and called us by name, so too may we recognize the value of each human life and pledge ourselves to continue to defend and nurture God's greatest gift to us.
-*NCCB 1992 Respect Life Manual*

The devil strains every nerve to secure the souls which belong to Christ. We should not grudge our toil in wresting them from Satan and giving them back to God. -*St. Sebastian*

The tempter, ever on the watch, wages war most violently against those whom he sees most careful to avoid sin.
-*Pope St. Leo the Great*

If there be a true way that leads to the Everlasting King-dom, it is most certainly that of suffering, patiently endured.
-*St. Colette*

Under the influence of fear, we bear the Cross of Christ with patience. Under the more inspiring influence of home, we carry the Cross with a firm and valiant heart. But under

91

the consuming power of love, we embrace the Cross with ardor.   *-St. Bernard*

Oh what remorse we shall feel at the end of our lives, when we look back upon the great number of instructions and examples afforded by God and the Saints for our perfection, and so carelessly received by us! If this end were to come to you today, how would you be pleased with the life you have led this year?   *-St. Francis de Sales*

Mary was raised to the dignity of Mother of God rather for sinners than for the just, since Jesus Christ declares that he came to call not the just, but sinners.   *-St. Anselm*

Of all divine things, the most godlike is to co-operate with God in the conversion of sinners.   *-St. Denis*

No matter how good food is, if poison is mixed with it, it may cause the death of him who eats it. So it is with conversation. A single bad word, an evil action, an unbecoming joke, is often enough to harm one or more young listeners, and may later cause them to lose God's grace.   *-St. John Bosco*

Let us avoid evil companions, lest by their company we may be drawn to a communion of vice.   *-St. Augustine*

When shall it be that we shall taste the sweetness of the Divine Will in all that happens to us, considering in everything only His good pleasure, by whom it is certain that adversity is sent with as much love as prosperity, and as much for our good? When shall we cast ourselves undeservedly into the arms of our most loving Father in Heaven, leaving to Him the care of ourselves and of our affairs, and reserving only the desire of pleasing Him, and of serving Him well in all that we can?   *-St. Jane Frances de Chantal*

Present sorrow and suffering is the way to glory, the way to the kingdom.   *-St. Bernard*

Our own evil inclinations are far more dangerous than any external enemies.

-St. Ambrose

He who walking on the sea could calm the bitter waves, who gives life to the dying seeds of the earth; he who was able to loose the mortal chains of death, and after three days' darkness could bring again to the upper world the brother for his sister Martha: he, I believe, will make Damasus rise again from the dust.

-St. Damasus (from an epitaph written for himself)

THE GLORIOUS MYSTERIES

First Glorious Mystery:

The Resurrection

"You need not be amazed! You are looking for Jesus of Nazareth, the one who was crucified. He has been raised up; he is not here. See the place where they laid him (Mark 16:6)."

It is early morning. Jesus' tomb remains sealed with wax, with reinforcements on either side of the heavy stone such that it is impossible to move except by several men or by first removing the reinforcement. Suddenly it happens! Without clear indication, without precedence, a most magnificent ball of immensely bright light appears in the heavens off to the east coming from whence no one knows, as if it were from the depths of the universe itself. It traverses the vast reaches of the heavens with such rapidity that it appears to be a comet.

There is the crack of thunder as the fireball races through the atmosphere. This is accompanied by a most unearthly thunder-like crescendo that seems to follow it as if warning of the impending crash that by now is imminent. This stirs even the overtired sleepy guards who, terrified by the thunderous roar, try to rise but fall due to a sudden unsettling quake of the earth. The guards, greatly disturbed interiorly as well as being visibly terrified, slowly try to find their feet. They try to flee the oncoming fireball.

The fireball slams ferociously into the huge rock blocking the tomb, and it is flung wildly aside as if it were but a pebble. The temple guards are knocked flat on the ground. The fireball eagerly enters the tomb, seeking its treasure; there it is, on the embalming table. After a few minutes the fireball begins to warm and excite the body, and the lifeless shape is illuminated, reaching great brilliance.

The new luminous body quickly sits up, and faster than the eye can follow, the brilliant form is standing upright just above the floor of the cave. As it dims slightly it takes shape; it appears to be a being of light, but it shines even brighter than many suns. Rays of still brighter light stream from the wounded hands and feet and side, and a lacework of pinpoints of light encircle the head. As the light dims slightly, a face becomes visible. Ah, this is indeed Him, this is the face of Jesus: how handsome and confident, not that of the vanquished, but the face of the conqueror.

Joyous and smiling, Jesus steps forward; there is eagerness within Him as He walks towards the entrance. Now there appear two more fiery figures with long trailing light golden hair, they are behind and to the sides of Jesus; heads bowed, they are kneeling, adoring the Savior of the World. Then the two angels rise, and one takes the cloth that had covered Jesus' head and reverently places it off to the side on a shelf. The other angel neatly rolls the cloth in which Jesus had been wrapped and leaves it on the embalming table.

Jesus walks forward, he is at the entrance to the cave now.

He does not bend in the least, He simply walks through the top stones of the cave lining into the bright morning sunshine and stops there. Jesus seems taller, His hair shines as strands of gold, his tunic is the most brilliant white; it seems to be woven of beams of light.

The Master, resplendent in His majestic heavenly attire looks at heaven and earth, His wandering gaze leaves out nothing. Loving and admiring, He drinks in the whole of His Father's creation. Jesus' sapphire blue eyes deepen the blue hue of the sky. Jesus looks upon all, caressing every detail. It is a caress of love from creator to creation.

Suddenly, without warning, without any warning whatever, the dazzling visitor from the depths of the universe disappears. The guards slowly rise again, thoroughly shaken, and seeing the brilliant light of angels they flee as fast as terror can compel them. The world looks the same, but it has been transformed forever, renewed forever. It is as if the horrors of the past days never happened. All is cleansed anew by the Light of the World.

Here we are reminded that Jesus is fully God and that He keeps His promises, all of them! He promised His mother and apostles and disciples and many others that He would rise from death. But only His mother Mary believed without doubt, all others thought the idea too radical, or too impossible. Did they fully believe Jesus was God? More importantly, do *we believe* that Jesus *is* fully God even though He was fully human? Do we believe that God the Father, Son, and Holy Spirit are present as one in the Eucharist? Do we understand that all three are the same in attributes, even in infinity of age?

Since we firmly believe through our eyes of faith that Jesus *is* God, let us strive to receive the Eucharist at every opportunity, and always on Saturdays and Sundays! This will help us join God's charity *to our will that is human charity*. The Eucharist will help us persist in holy desires; they are God's desires. Let us not worry about their imperfections, but try to keep pure motives! For God joins our holy works to His and makes them perfect!

Now reflect once again upon the great Resurrection mystery! See yourself standing outside the tomb on the morning of the Resurrection: Feel the cool breeze on your face, the birds are singing, the grass is wet with dew, you see the sun just beginning to come over the burial hill... you hear a noise like a train in the distance... the rock over the entrance to the tomb is gone and a light shines ever so brilliantly; in the center you see Jesus with His pierced hands and feet.

With a big smile Jesus embraces you and says, "I died for you..." Ask Jesus to let His resurrection power go to that part of you that needs healing, spiritually, emotionally, psychologically, relationally, even physically. Be open to the flow of resurrection power.

Holy enlightened One, King of heaven and earth, we humbly adore You in all Your splendor and majesty; light our paths with the rays of divine light emanating from Your most precious wounds. Have mercy on us, Jesus, forgive us our sins and lead us in Your light to Your new heavenly Jerusalem. Amen.

Second Glorious Mystery:

The Ascension

Then, after speaking to them, the Lord Jesus, was taken up into Heaven and took his seat at God's right hand (Mark 16:19).

It is morning, and the sunrise is rosy yellow and pink and red. Jesus is ready to ascend to Heaven, to go to His Father. Jesus and Mary have said all there is to say, now they are in deep contemplative exchanges of love. They know they part now for the last time, and pour out embraces and kisses of purest love. Then Mary, hair whipped in the light breeze, acknowledges her Son as God. She kneels in adoration before him for one last blessing, God-man and mother; and then Jesus lifts her up and kisses her one final time on her forehead.

Jesus takes His mother back to the house where the eleven have been staying. He greets them, blesses them, and admonishes them that His name will always be their blessing. He says they must be pure and holy in all things as they spread His kingdom across the world: one God, one Mystical body, one church. Jesus reminds them that Peter, the Supreme Pontiff and head of the Church, will be required to journey frequently, and thus the rest must remain together in His Spirit for the growth of His church. Jesus instructs them to love one another and never to get upset for any reason. For God knows all and allows only what is good in their spiritual journey, and He is with them wherever they are.

Jesus stands up; He is ready to go to the olive groves to meet the disciples. They embrace one another a last time, the apostles asking for Jesus' bread and His peace. Jesus lovingly smiles and blesses the bread and gives it to them. Then they all leave, Jesus walking alongside Mary and Peter and John. At the olive groves they are joined, forming a large crowd, by Lazarus and his sisters and Joseph and Nicodemus and the shepherds and so many others waiting for Jesus. Most believe, but some still doubt.

Jesus commissions them to go and make disciples of all nations, baptizing them… "And surely I am with you always, to the very end of this age (Matt 28:19-20)." Hundreds follow Jesus up the Mount of Olives. When Jesus reaches the chosen place He blesses all who are with Him, then He blesses the earth and sky and all living creatures, thanking them for the joy and comfort they gave Him. He even blesses the woods and thorns and hemp and metals and rocks that tortured Him in fulfilling His Father's will.

Jesus climbs further, to the summit, and He climbs on a large rock; He turns and faces the crowd. It is as if He looks individually at all of them at the same time. He opens His arms as if to embrace each of them; and then He tells them, "Go forth in my name and evangelize all the peoples of the earth. God be with you, go in peace. May His light lead your way, may His love comfort you always…" As Jesus is speaking He is transfigured before them, and His light becomes dazzling; He slowly raises His head towards His Father and rises.

The crowd kneels reverently as Jesus, resplendent in radiance and majesty, rises high into the sky and disappears into a cloud. Later they all stand, but it is clear they remain as in a daze, astonished at what they have just witnessed. Two angels appear, clad in white garments, and speak to the crowd, "Men of Galilee, why do you stand here looking into the sky? This same Jesus who has been taken from you into heaven, will come back in the same way you have seen Him go into heaven (Acts 1:11)."

We have just heard the everlasting question, "Why do you stand here looking into the sky?" How many times have we done that too! This very day *we have a great new opportunity*, "the rest of our lives." We can fulfill our Christian responsibilities; we can be that force for good, that "good Samaritan" to our neighbor, that evangelist for Jesus. We can avoid that critique of the two angels and be ready for Jesus when He comes for us.

Let us now envision this great mystery. See Jesus as He ascends into Heaven to go to the Father... He invites you to come with Him... Hold His hands after you give Him permission... Then Jesus takes you up with Him...going up...up...up... you go through the clouds and higher, up...up...and become one with Jesus...no longer two, but one...

All of a sudden, you are in the throne room... the Father is on a golden throne surrounded by Mary and her angels...He runs to you...He embraces you and kisses you and holds you in the air... This is My beloved son... daughter... receive My fatherly love that you did not receive from your earthly father... Absorb the love of the Father and be filled with His peace.

100

Dearest Jesus, we humbly and lovingly kneel before You as little children. We believe in You, adore You, trust You, love You, and thank You for Your many gifts, especially for Your warm loving presence in the most Holy Eucharist. Bread of life, nourish us; Blood of Christ, cleanse and renew us. Jesus we are yours forever! Amen.

Third Glorious Mystery

Descent of the Holy Spirit

All were filled with the Holy Spirit. They began to express themselves in foreign tongues and make bold proclamation as the Spirit prompted them (Acts 2:4).

Following Jesus' ascent into heaven, Mary and the apostles return to the house of the supper-room, while the disciples go their various ways. Days later the door is shut and the windows are barred, but Mary has the light of a candle with which to read the scrolls. Mary is sitting at a table with the apostles seated beside and opposite her. She is praying, and the apostles answer her invocations. She has an unusual smile of eagerness and anticipation. The apostles see this, but do not know why she smiles so mysteriously.

Suddenly there is the sound of a powerful wind roaring like a gigantic organ, deep and resonant and beautiful with a lighter sound like a stringed instrument that harmonizes with the deeper intonations. At this time… "There were staying in Jerusalem God-fearing Jews from every nation… When they heard this sound, a crowd came together in bewilderment because each one heard them speaking in his own language…" They said to one another, "We hear them declaring the wonders of God…" (Acts 2:5-11)

The apostles are frightened, but Mary puts her head back smiling in anticipation, fully knowing that her Son's promise is being fulfilled. Suddenly a brilliant sphere like a small sun but far more brilliant appears and moves over the head of Mary, and she goes into great joyful meditation breathing in the Holy Spirit of the Father and Son. The apostles look at her in amazement.

Then the fireball is broken, as was the body of Christ! Fire spins outward from the fireball forming fiery tongues that move over each of the apostles. The main fireball has reshaped itself into a crown-like ring which illuminates the head of Mary. The apostles' faces are transformed by the fire; they are immersed in a deep love and understanding of God. They are cleansed and refreshed, confident and bold. Peter speaks softly as Mary remains in heavenly joy, "I feel the fire of God burning in me, let us go out and proclaim the good news to the peoples of the world."

Scripture tells us that the Holy Spirit sanctifies us through wonderful gifts. The Holy Spirit does it in a most gentle loving way, as a cool soft breeze that will bend a reed but not break it. The Holy Spirit of the Father and His Son is eager to enlighten and empower us through His precious gifts. Why do we need these gifts? So all of us who are baptized go out into the world and heal the sick and preach the gospel as Jesus commanded! Note that Jesus' first mandate is to heal the sick; first in the soul, and then in the body. Healing the soul is far more important, because upon this rests eternal life!

Let us relive this great mystery. Picture yourself in the front of the room. It is long and narrow… twelve people are praying the psalms... it is getting warm as the sun shines through the windows... See the multi-colored turbans and vestments of the people rocking back and forth in prayer... You are kneeling between Mary and St. John... Mary says that she is praying for you that the Holy Spirit might give you a new gift of love for people... especially your family...

Suddenly there is the rush of wind blowing through the room cooling it down, and all the people feel it ... Mary places her hand on your shoulder and prays that the Holy Spirit might fill you in a new and more powerful way... See the tongues of fire over the people and yourself... watch as the fire enters the heart of each person... Feel the heat in your own heart... Feel the Holy Spirit encapsulating you in His love.

Eternal Father and Son, send the fire of your Holy Spirit into my heart that I may know You, love You, and serve You; and that I may make You known and loved across the world. Holy Spirit of God, breathe on me that I may become a perfect reflection of Jesus. Lord God Jesus, may I heal souls and bodies in Your name through Your most precious body and blood. Amen; and amen; and amen!

Fourth Glorious Mystery:

The Assumption of Mary

You are the glory of Jerusalem... you are the splendid boast of our people... God is pleased with what you have wrought. May you be blessed by the Lord Almighty forever and ever (Judith 15:9-10).

Mary lived the remaining years of her long life with John, the beloved disciple, near Gethsemane in one of the country houses of Lazarus. She had grown old in years, but her beauty had not faded. See her now; she is slim like Jesus but not nearly so tall. She looks as if she were still in her early thirties. Her lovely hair cascades across her shoulders, her delightful blue eyes are like beautiful sapphires, and her nose and mouth are small and beautiful.

When Mary smiles at you, it is as though the sun warms and caresses you in purest love and joy, and you feel great peace. John has become so enamored with her holy presence that he dreads her passing. But he is greatly comforted as he knows in his heart that she will never undergo death as most of us do; that she who was without sin will joyously pass on to heaven right into the arms of God. There she will attain to perfect adoration, beatitude, peace, enlightenment, and exultation of light...

Mary has been the mother of the church on earth, and she worked with the apostles as they fulfilled their mission of evangelizing the world. She humbly accepted and deeply loved Peter, appointed by Jesus as the Supreme Pontiff of the church. She suffered greatly as so many of her friends including most of Jesus' apostles and disciples were martyred for the faith.

Mary has grown weary through the dark days of the great struggle to overcome the myriad of obstacles to the church, feeling that she can be of greater help now in heaven than on earth. The blood of the martyrs has made fertile the spiritual ground on which the church is to grow strong and faithful to the Truth that is Christ Jesus, Our Lord. She sees the faith spreading across Israel into neighboring countries.

John contemplates all this, day after day; and seeing Mary grow more pale he feels the time of her departure is ever near. He felt from reading scripture that God would take this innocent dove to Abraham's bosom in an extraordinary way. He wants to enjoy this great event so that he will not be left quite so bereft and destitute. John now feels the time is imminent, so he refuses to sleep; he lies there in vigil at night waiting patiently. Three days pass like this and then, totally exhausted, he falls into a deep sleep.

Mary, who knows that the time has come, prays as she lies motionless on her bed. She is very tired. She prays and prays until she is fully possessed by the Holy Spirit. Excitement and anticipation grow in her soul, and a smile appears on her face. Her soul leaves her body, rising towards heaven. Mary breathes her last. Her guardian angel has eagerly awaited this moment, and he summons a great host of angels, even from the highest heaven. John sees none of this, as he is sound asleep.

The ceiling of Mary's room has vanished! Suddenly there appear in Mary's room and above many legions of angels, brilliantly clad in light. The angels surround Mary's bed, pick up her lifeless body, and begin lifting it upward into the sky; it is a long procession of brilliant light and even brighter figures of light. The procession upward sounds like a gigantic organ with strings pricked all in a melodious pattern, and it is mixed with the singing of angels. As they rise higher and higher, the sound begins to fade below in the house. The roof of the house reappears, and all is peaceful.

But John was awakened by the loud music, and with spiritual eyes he "saw" all that was happening. Mary is gone, but God has made it possible for this pure man to envision Mary as she continues to be raised towards heaven. John sees Mary's soul rejoin and animate her body as it is transformed into a being of greater beauty and light, and she stands up smiling joyously. Now her glorified body is drawn upward by Jesus without the aid of angels. Jesus comes down from heaven to greet her, and they embrace in indescribable beauty and purity of love and joy.

We know that Mary was conceived without sin. But what pleased the Father so much was that Mary served Him with all her heart, that she never once in the least strayed from doing His Holy Will. Mary emulated Jesus perfectly; and she often prayed lying face-down on the floor. Mary fasted and sang canticles of praise as she worked.

After Joseph's death, Mary followed Jesus' example, eating an evening meal only. Thus Mary was born pure and holy and most beautiful to heaven itself, and she remained such throughout life, retaining an incorruptible body and soul. Her holy actions excited the angels, and she was their great joy.

Neither her physical nor her spiritual beauty was ever diminished at any time in any way.

Picture yourself in a small room with practically no light except a candle on a table where Mary has just breathed her last. She is not there in bed, for she has been raised up... She is no longer there... But you can see her in your spirit being assumed by God the Father, the Son, and their Holy Spirit to Heaven... See all three persons of the Trinity welcome her ... see Mary crowned with great sensitivities and charity and powers...and hear Mary and her angels sing and rejoice. Pure and good and beautiful, Mary reflects God so perfectly!

Mary calls *you* to merit Heaven by your good life and virtue... She says, "Pray for your family to join you in Heaven for all eternity." Pray with Mary for the salvation of the world. Mary prays intensely with tears of blood, that not more than a third of mankind will fall into the eternal clutch of Satan, for John who saw the last days said, "...and with his tail he drew after him a third of the stars and made them fall (Revelation 12:14)."

Think of one great weakness you have, and ask Mary to pray for that... and think of the one member of your family, who needs healing the most. Pray for that person, and ask Mary to intercede on behalf of that person. Mary will hold you and your family up to her Son in prayer. But you should also ask for it!

Most holy lady of Heaven, I thank you for bearing the Son of the Most High God. Through humble faith and hope and love you gave birth to redemption itself through your Son, Jesus Christ. Help us, Mary, to obtain the grace to aid you and Jesus in the greater redemption of mankind.

Fifth Glorious Mystery:

The Coronation of Mary

A great sign appeared in the sky, a woman clothed with the sun, with the moon under her feet, and on her head a crown of twelve stars (Revelation 12:1).

Mary and Jesus and the angels rise ever higher towards heaven, and Mary's beauty is made perfect by an inexpressible joy. As they approach the New Heavenly Jerusalem, they are joined by Mary's earthly spouse Joseph, and by all the just kings and patriarchs and first martyrs and saints of the church.

Our Eternal Father is there with His Holy Spirit to greet them. Jesus presents his mother Mary to His Heavenly Father, and there is an embrace of indescribable love; and then the Father presents Mary to His Holy Spirit, and Mary is filled with the "all" of God. She has everything! Now not only is God in Mary, "but now Mary is in God" too!

This all happens within the splendor and celestial beauty of remarkable heavenly colors and sights and sounds that remain unknowable to man, but are perfectly delightful to all the angels and just souls. As Mary is now in God, she receives inconceivable gifts of the attributes of God, as she is His perfect reflection. How can we ever forget this great event! Consider the sun which warms our earth and is reflected by the moon; the sun is our earthly reminder of Jesus, the sustainer of life; and the moon is the reminder of His ever-virgin mother, reflecting the light and love of God for His human family.

Following Jesus' death, Mary heroically assisted the church that He had given birth to. Today, Mary is present at every mass in every country of the world, coming early to heal souls and to prepare the congregation for the great liturgical and sacramental miracle of the mass. Holy Mary is our mother, our intercessor and our protector. She is the fountain of knowledge and an ocean of mercy, overflowing with grace.

When we are lonely, in pain, exhausted, or in utter despair, Mary comes to us with our eternal angel Jesus even before we call. Through the mysterious workings of the Holy Spirit, Jesus and Mary give us comfort and consolation, and they lift our spirits to their breasts. They embrace us in eternal love, bestowing immeasurable blessings upon us.

We must support Jesus' church too, as did Mary. Our time and talents and finances are all god-given, and it is fitting and proper to tithe a tenth of what we have to charity. Jesus said, "Give to Ceasar what is Ceasar's, and to God what is God's." In the hour of our death, when we are utterly helpless, we need the support and comfort of our guardian angel and Joseph and Mary and Jesus. How better to engender their support than to help them while we still can!

Are we doing what we can for our church? Do we support our priests and deacons and nuns, our choir, our program directors, our catechetical personnel, and all the others who make our church a living member of the mystical body of Christ? Do we act on opportunities given to us to evangelize?

In meditating on Mary's Assumption and Coronation, we see that Jesus' mother was the first and only human to reach God's throne in her glorified body, though this was the original creative thought for all souls. Following Jesus' ascension, Mary had received the Eucharist daily. Through this holy union with God, her soul had desired more and more the embrace of God *unveiled*.

As the end of her life approached, every time she received the Eucharist, Mary heard the faint call of her Son as He whispered ever so softly, "Mother, come to me." Mary felt her bonds to the earth weaken while her desire to be *in God* intensified and burned within her. More and more Mary was drawn towards her eternal home, towards her everlasting love, her Father God.

Mary's message for our time is a request for greater prayer. The world is in terrible sin, and the just hand of the Father has grown heavy, not to punish, but to *correct* that we might not be lost. Our Father wishes that we revere Him and, above all, that we grow close to Him so that we confidently trust in Him. From Our Father proceeds all that was, is, and will be. He is our refuge, our hope, and our fatherland. Join Mary as she glorifies God, repeating softly, "Praise be to Jesus, now and forever!"

Envision now the coronation of Mary. See her standing with Jesus; the Father and the Holy Spirit are also present. Hear Mary as she calls *you* forth, "Come," she says quietly, "Let me embrace you, and give you a mother's love." Some of you missed that love from your earthly mother... Go to Mary's throne and let her hug you and pray for you. Feel her motherly love flow into you and give you a deep sense of being loved as a child... Let your inner child ask to be open to all that is possible in this beautiful moment... lean against her chest and be encapsulated within her motherly affection that heals.

Mary, most holy Lady of Heaven, we love and revere you as Our Mother and Our Queen! Pray with us for the grace to grow in the knowledge and love of God that we may live a holier life. Mary, pray for us, intercede for us, and help us at the hour of our death. Amen.

Glorious Reflections of Saints

Mary stayed outside the tomb weeping. And as she wept, she bent over into the tomb and saw two angels in white sitting there, one at the head and one at the feet where the body of Jesus had been. And they said to her, "Woman, why are you weeping?" She said to them, "They have taken my Lord, and I don't know where they laid him." When she had said this, she turned around and saw Jesus there, but did not know it was Jesus.   *-Jn 20:11-14*

...She thought it was the gardener and said to him, "Sir, if you carried him away, tell me where you laid him, and I will take him." Jesus said to her, "Mary!" She turned and said to him in Hebrew. "Rabbouni," which means Teacher. Jesus said to her, "Stop holding on to me, for I have not yet ascended to the Father. But go to my brothers and tell them, 'I am going to my Father and your Father, to my God and your God.' Mary of Magdala went and announced to the disciples, "I have seen the Lord," and what he told her.   *-Jn 20:11-18*

Having confidence in you, O Mother of God, I shall be saved. Being under your protection, I shall fear nothing. With you help I shall give battle to my enemies and put them to flight; for devotion to you is an arm of salvation.

-St. John Damascene

As every mandate of grace that is sent by a king passes through the palace gates, so does every grace that comes from Heaven to the world pass through the hands of Mary.

-St. Bernard

O Holy Mary! My Mother; into your blessed trust and special custody, and into the bosom of your mercy, I this day, and every day, and in the hour of my death, commend my soul and my body. To you I commit all my anxieties and sorrows, my life and the end of my life, that by your mot holy intercession, and my your merits, all my actions may be directed and governed by your will and that of your Son. Amen.

-St. Aloysius Gonzaga

Courage, my sons, don't you see that we are leaving on a mission? They pay our fare in the bargain. What a piece of good luck! The thing to do now is to pray well in order to win as many souls as possible. Let us, then, tell the Blessed Virgin that we are content, and that she can do with us anything she wishes.

-St. Maximilian Kolbe

Mary was raised to the dignity of Mother of God rather for sinners than for the just, since Jesus Christ declares that he came to call not the just, but sinners.

-St. Anselm

When our hands have touched spices, they give fragrance to all they handle. Let us make our prayers pass through the hands of the Blessed Virgin. She will make them fragrant.

-St. John Vianney

Believe me, the writing of pious books, the composing of the most sublime poetry; all that does not equal the smallest act of self-denial.

-St. Therese of Lisieux

God is love, and all his operations proceed from love. Once he wills to manifest that goodness by sharing his love outside himself, then the Incarnation becomes the supreme manifestation of his goodness and love and glory. So, Christ was intended before all other creatures and for his own sake. For him all things were created and to him all things must be subject, and God loves all creatures in and because of Christ. Christ is the first-born of every creature, and the whole of humanity as well as the created world finds its foundation and meaning in him. Moreover, this would have been the case even if Adam had not sinned.   *-St. Lawrence of Brindisi*

We must love our neighbor as being made in the image of God and as an object of His love.   *-St. Vincent de Paul*

Love consumes us only in the measure of our self-surrender.   *-St. Therese of Lisieux*

Whoever does not love does not know God. Why? Because God is Love. What more can be said, my Brothers? If one did not find one word in praise of love through this epistle, nor the least word through out all the other pages of Scripture, and we heard only this one word from the voice of the Spirit of God: Because 'God is Love,' we should seek for nothing more.
-St. Augustine from his commentary on the First Epistle of St. John.

We must love our neighbor as being made in the image of God and as an object of His love.   *-St. Vincent de Paul*

God bestows more consideration on the purity of the intention with which our actions are performed than on the actions themselves.   *-St. Augustine*

True charity consists in putting up with all one's neighbor's faults, never being surprised by his weakness, and being inspired by the least of his virtues.   *-St. Therese of Lisieux*

Prayer should be accomplished by grace and not by artifice.   *-St. Jane Frances de Chantal*

Think well. Speak well. Do well. These three things, through the mercy of God, will make a man go to Heaven.
-St. Camillus de Lellis

Just as we can never separate asceticism from mysticism, so in St. John of the Cross we find darkness and light, suffering and joy, sacrifice and love united together so closely that they seem at times to be identified.   *-Thomas Merton*

Thomas, called Didymus, one of the Twelve, was not with them when Jesus came. So the other disciples said to him, "We have seen the Lord." But he said to them, "Unless I see the mark of the nails in his hands and put my finger into the nail marks and put my hand into his side, I will not believe." Now a week later his disciples were again inside and Thomas was with them. Jesus came, although the doors were locked, and stood in their midst and said, "Peace be with you." Then he said to Thomas, "Put your finger here and see my hands, and bring your hand and put it into my side, and do not be unbelieving, but believe." Thomas answered and said to him, "My Lord and my God!" Jesus said to him, "Have you come to believe because you have not seen me? Blessed are those who have not seen and have believed."   *-Jn 20:24-29*

Lay me not with sweet spices,
For this honor avails me not,
Nor yet use incense and perfumes,
For the honor befits me not.
Burn yet the incense in the holy place;
As for me, escort me only with your prayers,
Give your incense to God,
And over me send up hymns.
Instead of perfumes and spices,
Be mindful of me in you intercessions.   *-St. Ephrem*

No sacrifice is more acceptable to God than zeal for souls.
                                        -*St. Gregory the Great*

Our Lord needs from us neither great deeds nor profound thoughts. Neither intelligence nor talents. He cherishes simplicity.   -*St. Thérèse of Lisieux*

Dear Lord, you know my weakness. Each morning I resolve to be humble, and in the evening I recognize that I have often been guilty of pride. The sight of these faults tempts me to discouragement. Yet I know that discouragement itself is a form of pride. I wish, therefore, O my God, to build all my trust upon You. As You can do all things, deign to implant in my soul this virtue which I desire.   -*St. Therese of Lisieux*

She seeks for those who approach her devoutly and with reverence, for she loves, nourishes, and adopts as her children.   -*St. Bonaventure*

The air that we breathe, the bread that we eat, the heart which throbs in our bosoms, are not more necessary for man that he may live as a human being, than is prayer for the Christian that he may live as a Christian.   -*St. John Eudes*

Prayer is to our soul what rain is to the soil. Fertilize the soil ever so richly, it will remain barren unless fed by frequent rains.   -*St. John Vianney*

No one should judge that he has greater perfection because he performs great penances and gives himself in excess to the staying of the body than he who does less, inasmuch as neither virtue or merit consists therein; for otherwise he would be an evil case, who for some legitimate reason was unable to do actual penance. Merit consists in the virtue of love alone, flavored with the light of true discretion, without which the soul is worth nothing.
                                      -*St. Catherine of Siena*

Pray with great confidence, with confidence based upon the promises of Jesus Christ. God is a spring of living water which flows unceasingly into the hearts of those who pray.

-St. Louis de Montfort

You will not see anyone who is really striving after his advancement who is not given to spiritual reading. And as to him who neglects it, the fact will soon be observed by his progress.

-St. Athanasius

Prayer reveals to souls the vanity of earthly goods and pleasures. It fills them with light, strength and consolation; and gives them a foretaste of the calm bliss of our heavenly home.

-St. Rose of Viterbo

There is no doubt that through the reading of the Sacred Scriptures the soul is set aflame in God and becomes purified from all vices.

-St. Jerome

Why do you not use the time when you have nothing to do for reading or for prayer? Why do you not go and visit Christ our Lord and speak with Him and listen to Him? For when we pray we speak with God, and when we read, we listen to God.

-St. Ambrose

Faith believes, hope prays, and charity begs in order to give to other. Humility of the heart forms the prayer, confidence speaks it, and perseverance triumphs over God Himself.

-St. Peter Julian Eymard

Those who are pure are temples of the Holy Spirit.

-St. Lucy

Cast down upon us a glance of mercy, O most glorious Queen: graciously receive our petitions. Through thy immaculate purity of body and mind, which rendered thee so pleasing to God, inspire us with a love of innocence and purity.

-St. Paschasius

Love Mary!... She is loveable, faithful, constant. She will never let herself be outdone in love, but will ever remain supreme. If you are in danger, she will hasten to free you. If you are troubled, she will console you. If you are sick, she will bring you relief. If you are in need, she will help you. She does not look to see what kind of person you have been. She simply comes to a heart that wants to love her. She comes quickly and opens her merciful heart to you, embraces you and consoles and serves you. She will even be at hand to accompany you on the trip to eternity.

-St. Gabriel of the Sorrowful Mother.

I am the Immaculate Conception.

*-Revelation of the Virgin Mary to
St. Bernadette at Lourdes.*

To be pleased at correction and reproofs shows that one loves the virtues which are contrary to those faults for which he is corrected and reproved. And, therefore, it is a great sign of advancement in perfection. *-St. Francis de Sales*

Give yourself in earnest to the acquisition of virtue; otherwise, you will remain always a dwarf in it. Never believe that you have acquired a virtue, if you have not made proof of it in resisting its contrary vice, and unless you practice it faithfully on suitable occasions which, for this reason, ought never to be avoided, but rather desired, sought, and embraced with eagerness. *-St. Teresa*

O Mary, I wash always to be thy child. I give thee my heart; keep it thine for ever. *-St. Dominic Savio*

O how long since would the world have been destroyed had not Mary sustained it by her powerful intercession.

- St. Fulgentius

Prayer is the bulwark of chastity. *-St. Gregory the Great*

How beautiful it is to behold a person destitute of all attachment, ready for any act of virtue or charity, gentle to all, indifferent as to any employment, serene in consolations and tribulations, and wholly content if only the will of God is done! *-St. Francis de Sales*

There is something in humility that strangely exalts the heart. *-St. Augustine*

Vigilance and prayer are the safeguards of chastity. You should pray often and fervently to be preserved from temptations against purity, and for the grace to overcome them. *-St. John Baptist de la Salle*

You ask me a method of attaining perfection. I know of love - and only love. Love can do all things. *-St. Therese of Lisieux*

To love God is something greater than to know Him. *-St. Thomas Aquinas*

It is not the actual physical exertion that counts toward a man's progress, nor the nature of the task, but the spirit of faith with which it is undertaken. *-St. Francis Xavier*

See what love does, when it is true. If we loved God truly, we should do as much for all our neighbors who are sons of God, and resemble him much. *-St. Francis de Sales*

O Mary, conceived without sin, pray for us who have recourse to thee. *-Words on the Miraculous Medal revealed to Catherine Laboure*

Charity unites us to God... There is nothing mean in charity, nothing arrogant. Charity knows no schism, does not rebel, does all things in concord. In charity all the elect of God have been made perfect. *-Pope St. Clement I*

"Who will praise the blessed Lea as she deserves? She renounced painting her face and adorning her head with shining pearls. She exchanged her rich attire for sackcloth and ceased to command others in order to obey all. She dwelt in a corner with a few bits of furniture; she spent her nights in prayer and instructed her companions through her example rather than through protests and speeches. And she looked forward to her arrival in heaven in order to receive her recompense for the virtues which she practiced on earth. "So it is that thenceforth she enjoyed perfect happiness. From Abraham's bosom, where she resides with Lazarus, she sees our consul who was once decked out in purple now vested in a shameful robe, vainly begging for a drop of water to quench his thirst. Although he went up to the capital to the plaudits of the people, and his death occasioned widespread grief, it is futile for the wife to assert that he has gone to heaven and possesses a great mansion there. The fact is that he is plunged into the darkness outside Whereas Lea who was willing to be considered a fool on earth has been received into the house of the Father, at the wedding feast of the Lamb. "Hence, I tearfully beg you to refrain from seeking the favors of the world and to renounce all that is carnal. It is impossible to follow both the world and Jesus. Let us live a life of renunciation, for our bodies will soon be dust and nothing else will last any longer."   -*St. Jerome*

When they had gathered together they asked him, "Lord, are you at this time going to restore the kingdom to Israel?" He answered them, "It is not for you to know the times or seasons that the Father has established by his own authority. But you will receive power when the Holy Spirit comes upon you, and you will be my witnesses in Jerusalem, throughout Judea and Samaria, and to the ends of the earth." When he had said this, as they were looking on, he was lifted up and a cloud took him from their sight. While there were looking intently at the sky as he was going, suddenly two men dressed in white garments stood beside them. They said, "Men of Galilee, why are you standing there looking at the sky? This Jesus who has been taken up from you into heaven will return in the same way as you have seen him going into heaven." They returned to Jerusalem from the mount called Olivet, which is near Jerusalem, a Sabbath day's journey away.

-Acts 1:6-12

While they were still speaking about this, he stood in their midst and said to them, "Peace be with you." But they were startled and terrified and thought that they were seeing a ghost. Then he said to them, "Why are you troubled? And why do questions arise in your hearts? Look at my hands and my feet, that is I myself. Touch me and see, because a ghost does not have flesh and bones as you can see I have. And as he said this, he showed them his hands and his feet. Then beginning with Moses and all the prophets, he interpreted to them what referred to him in all the scriptures. As they approached the village to which they were going, he gave the impression that he was going on farther. But they urged him, "Stay with us, for it is nearly evening and the day is almost over." So he went in to stay with them. And it happened that, while he was at table, he took bread, said the blessing, broke it, and gave it to them. With that their eyes were opened and they recognized him, but he vanished from their sight. Then they said to each other, "Were not our hearts burning while he spoke to us on the way and opened the scriptures to us?" So they set out at once and returned to Jerusalem where they found gathered together the eleven and those with them who were saying, "The Lord has truly been raised and has appeared to Simon!" Then the two recounted what had taken place on the way and how he was made known to them in the breaking of the bread.

-Lk 24:27-35

Appendix 1

Dedicated in utmost love and honor of Jesus' birth, life, passion, death and resurrection.

The LITANY of "Jesus, Prisoner of Love"

Blessed be Jesus, Prisoner of sinners,
    Forgive our sins.
Blessed be Jesus, Prisoner of unbelievers,
    Forgive our unbelief.
Blessed be Jesus, Prisoner for souls,
    Save us.
Blessed be Jesus, Prisoner for redemption's sake,
    Redeem us.
Blessed be Jesus, Prisoner in agony,
    Help us in distress.
Blessed be Jesus, Prisoner of mockery,
    Bless those who mock us.
Blessed be Jesus, Prisoner of the temple,
    Pray for us.
Blessed be Jesus, Prisoner of Pilate,
    Have mercy on judges.

Blessed be Jesus, Prisoner of Herod,
   Have mercy on governors.

Blessed be Jesus, Prisoner of scourging,
   Have mercy on those who strike us.

Blessed be Jesus, Prisoner of thorns,
   Have mercy on those who pierce our hearts.

Blessed be Jesus, Prisoner of nails,
   Have mercy on those who pierce our souls.

Blessed be Jesus, Prisoner of the cross,
   Have mercy on those who torture us.

Blessed be Jesus, Prisoner of the unmerciful,
   Have compassion on the merciful.

Blessed be Jesus, Prisoner of unforgiveness,
   Forgive our sins.

Blessed be Jesus, Prisoner of pain,
   Heal us.

Blessed be Jesus, Prisoner unconsoled,
   Console us.

Blessed be Jesus, Prisoner of sorrow,
   Comfort us.

Blessed be Jesus, Prisoner for love's sake,
   Help us to love.

Blessed be Jesus, Prisoner of Your mother's heart,
   Grant us Your mother's love.

Blessed be Jesus, Prisoner in the Most Blessed
   Sacrament,
   Draw us to life everlasting.

Blessed be Jesus, Prisoner in the Most Holy Tabernacle,
   Grant us your refuge.

Blessed be Jesus, Prisoner in the Monstrance,

Receive our prayers.

Blessed be Jesus, Prisoner of our hearts,
Dwell in us.

Blessed be Jesus, Word of God,
Enlighten us.

Blessed be Jesus, Son of Our Father,
Make us heirs of heaven.

Blessed be Jesus, Love of the Spirit,
Show us your Sacred Heart.

Jesus, Blest of the Trinity,
Unite our heart with yours.

Jesus, Lord, have mercy on us.

Jesus, Lord, have mercy on us.

Jesus Christ, have mercy on us,

Jesus Christ, have mercy on us,

Jesus, Lord, have mercy on us and on the whole world.

Jesus, Lord, have mercy on us and on the whole world.

References

1. All Scriptures taken from *Saint Joseph Edition of* The *New American* Bible. Copyright © 1992 by Catholic Book Publishing Co., New York.
2. All Reflections taken from *Quotes of Saints* from website: bend@liturgical.com.
3. Five Sorrowful and First Glorious stories taken from the manuscript *We Are Saved*. Copyright ©2003 by Eugene Peter Koshenina, 17 Oak Harbor Drive, Houston, Texas 77062.
4. Partial texts of each mystery taken from the text of *Healing Through The Rosary* 2-CD set. Copyright © 2000 by Fr. Robert DeGrandis, S.S.J. and Cecilia, 17 Oak Harbor Drive, Houston, Texas 77062.

Books
by
Father Robert DeGrandis, S.S.J.

The Gift of Miracles $8.00

Healing Through the Mass $8.00

The Word of Knowledge $7.00

Praying for Miracles $7.00

Called to Serve (a new title of Come Follow Me) $7.00

Healing the Broken Heart $6.00

Intergenerational Healing $6.00

Resting in the Spirit $6.00

Renewed by the Holy Spirit $6.00

The Gift of Prophecy $5.00

Layperson's Manual for the Healing Ministry $5.00

Growing in Jesus $5.00

To Forgive Is Divine $5.00

Coming to Life $3.00

The Power of Healing Prayer $3.00

The Gift of Tongues $3.00

Inner Healing Through the Stations of the Cross $3.00

Forgiveness and Inner Healing $3.00

Self-Image (Healing Life's Emotions) $3.00

A New Introduction of the Catholic Charismatic
   Renewal $3.00

Healing and Catholics $3.00

The Ten Commandments of Prayer $3.00

By a Miracle, They were Changed Forever $3.00

Young People's Forgiveness Prayer $2.00

Forgiveness Is Healing (The Forgiveness Prayer) $2.00

Testimony of Father Robert DeGrandis, S.S.J. $2.00

Healing the Father Relationship $2.00

Integrating Healing Into the Parish $2.00
Introduction to Inner Healing $2.00
Failure in Your Life $2.00
Receiving Holy Eucharist, the Road to Healing $2.00
Charisms $2.00
Mary Mother Salt of the Earth $2.00
Praising God Daily $2.00
To Love Is to Forgive $2.00
The Real Presence $4.00
Pray Your Way to Happiness $4.00
Spiritual Healing of the Family $4.00

Audio Books & Albums
by Father Robert DeGrandis, S.S.J.

Complete Teaching on the Gifts (12 tapes) $40.00
Healing Gifts of the Holy Spirit (6 tapes) $26.00
The Gifts of the Holy Spirit (6 tapes) $26.00
Maturing in the Gifts (4 tapes) $16.00
God is Love (4 tapes) $16.00
Set Free (4 tapes) $16.00
Spiritual Gifts (4 tapes) $16.00
Healing of Memories (4 tapes) $16.00
Healing of Ancestors (4 tapes) $16.00
Healing the Family (4 tapes) $16.00
Guidelines for Leaders (4 tapes) $16.00
Healing Through Hearing the Word (4 tapes) $16.00
Healing of Self-Image (3 tapes) $12.00
Healing Through the Mass (1 tape) .... $ 6.00
Healing Through the Rosary (1 tape) .... $ 8.00
Basics of Healing (1 tape) .... $ 6.00